MATH

LESSONS FOR A LIVING EDUCATION

Level 1

Angela O'Dell

MASTERBOOKS® CURRICULUM

Author: Angela O'Dell

Master Books Creative Team:

Editor: Craig Froman

Design: Terry White

Cover Design: Diana Bogardus

Copy Editors: Judy Lewis

Curriculum Review:
Kristen Pratt
Laura Welch
Diana Bogardus

First printing: March 2016
Seventh printing: August 2020

ISBN: 978-0-89051-923-3
ISBN: 978-1-61458-488-9 (digital)

Images are from shutterstock.

Unless otherwise noted, Scripture quotations are from the New King James Version of the Bible.

Printed in the United States of America

Please visit our website for other great titles:

www.masterbooks.com

Dedication

For all of the precious children, the ability to learn is a gift from God.

Author Bio:

As a homeschooling mom and author, **Angela O'Dell** embraces many aspects of the Charlotte Mason method yet knows that modern children need an education that fits the needs of this generation. Based upon her foundational belief in a living God for a living education, she has worked to bring a curriculum that will reach deep into the heart of home-educated children and their families. She has written over 20 books, including her history series and her math series. Angela's goal is to bring materials that teach and train hearts and minds to find the answers for our generation in the never-changing truth of God and His Word.

Scope and Sequence

Using This Course

Features: The suggested weekly schedule enclosed has easy-to-manage lessons that guide the reading, worksheets, and all assessments. The pages of this course are perforated and three-hole punched so materials are easy to tear out, hand out, grade, and store. Teachers are encouraged to adjust the schedule and materials needed in order to best work within their unique educational program.

Lesson Scheduling: "Quizzes" or reviews (whichever you want to use them as) are in the form of "letters to Mom and Dad." The twins want to show their parents what they have been learning on Grandpa and Grandma's farm, and they need your students to help them! Your students show what they have learned by writing the letters for the twins. The last 6 lessons are focused reviews, covering topics learned throughout the first 30 lessons.

🕐	Approximately 30 minutes per lesson, five days a week, for 36 weeks
🔑	Answer keys for worksheets are available online: www.masterbooks.com/classroom-aids
📑	Worksheets are included for each section
📄	Designed for grade 1 in a one-year course

Course Description

This book was written to be used by you and your young student together. It is the story of a twin brother and sister who are visiting their grandparents' farm. They soon learn that the farm is full of learning opportunities! As you read their story, your student will be drawn into the adventure along with the twins. They will learn about numbers, shapes, place value, adding, and subtracting. They will also learn about gardening, baby animals on the farm, nature, and the love of family. They will hear exciting stories from Grandpa and Grandma, and they will be invited to join the twins on their living math adventures. I hope you have a grand time on this adventure. Below is an explanation of how this book is laid out. It is meant to be easy to use and something students will want to do every day. Have a wonderful time exploring and learning!

The first 30 lessons each have a story about the twins, followed by a lesson taught by Grandpa or Grandma through hands-on learning around the farm. Sometimes this lesson is learned by the twins' explorations in nature. After the story, there is a section for your students to practice the lesson they learned, and to review what they have learned earlier.

Note: You can supplement the worksheets in the *Math for a Living Education* series with additional worksheets, activities, and quizzes in *Practice Makes Perfect*, also available from Master Books.

Students completing this course will

- ✓ Learn their numbers from 0 to 100
- ✓ Review circles and patterns, counting and addition, days of the week, and telling time
- ✓ Explore simple concepts and symbols used in mathematics, and simple fractions
- ✓ Identify place values, number families, and solving for an unknown.

How can mathematics be taught as a living subject?

Have you ever noticed that we tend to compartmentalize when teaching our children? In real life, there aren't artificial barriers between "subjects." For example, when you are cooking or baking, you have to use the skills of reading, logical thinking, and measuring, just to name a few. In driving a car, you see and read road signs, read maps, and count miles. So why do we say to our students, "This is math, this is language, this is science/nature, this is history. . . ?"

I have learned that it is most natural and most effective to teach children, not subjects. For example, one conversation, which was originally about telling time, turned into a story about when I was a child and completely burned a batch of cookies because I didn't set a timer. Out came the timer, which was scrutinized closely by all within hearing. Out came the cookbook, which was carefully perused by two sisters, who decide they would like to make cookies and remember to set the timer. Little sister asked if she could help by measuring, and Mom said, "You know, guys, while you are making the cookies, I will play the audio book CD that we started last night!"

In this story, what if I had said, "NO, we are sticking to telling time, and we are going to drill about how to learn to tell time!" A wonderful chance to bring math to life would have slipped by. Even more sadly, the children would not have the chance to actually use the skill. They would have missed the opportunity to see how telling time is only part of the picture — they would have missed out on why telling time is important for them to learn, and how it can help them in everyday life.

I am not saying that there aren't times to stick to the topic on hand, and I most certainly am not saying that there isn't a time and place for drill. But drill cannot take the place of math in real life. One without the other is like love without discipline or discipline without love. We have to have balance! It has become quite clear to me that there is an abundance of math curriculums available that are nothing but monotonous drill sheets dressed up in pretty colors. Pretty colors do not make a living book. Content, story, and the ability to show math in real life make a living math book.

Now Available

Supply list for manipulatives

In the back of the book, you will find a manipulatives section. Before starting the book, gather these resources.

- ☐ contact paper and construction paper
- ☐ large index cards
- ☐ brass fasteners
- ☐ crayons, markers, and colored pencils
- ☐ glue or paste
- ☐ hole punch and hole reinforcers
- ☐ rings to keep flashcards together
- ☐ a plastic shoebox with lid in which to store manipulatives

- ☐ (optional but helpful) stickers to use for flashcards
- ☐ pictures from old magazines
- ☐ poster board (several large pieces)
- ☐ at least 100 "counting items" (dried beans, buttons, and craft sticks all work well)
- ☐ 3 containers for your Place Value Village (1 larger, 1 medium, 1 smaller)
- ☐ snack-size baggies, and one durable gallon-or quart-size freezer bag

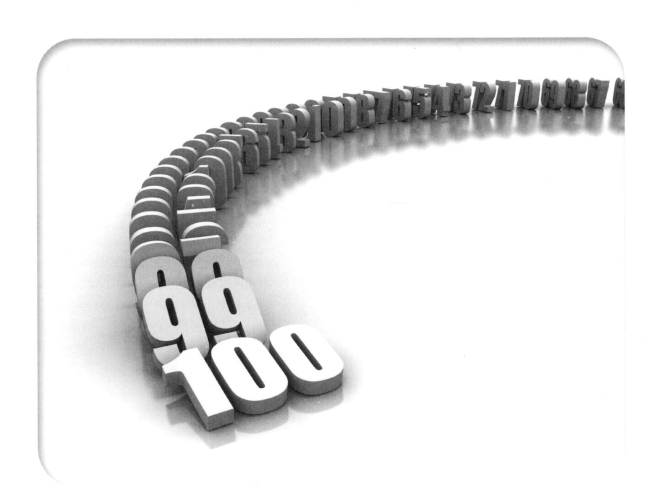

How to use everyday items as manipulatives

Contrary to popular opinion, you don't need fancy, expensive, special manipulatives to teach math concepts. What? As shocking as that is, I can personally attest that it is 100 percent true; I've been doing it for years. So how do you turn all those small items that hang around your house and fill your "junk drawer" into useful math manipulatives?

Well, let's start with my favorite, the trusty dried bean*! When you are teaching your students place value, dried beans just might become your new best friends. How? Follow these steps:

1. When your student is counting 0–9, simply place single beans into the ONE'S house, and have your student write on their Place Value Village Mat, the numbers 0–9.

2. As we all know, only 9 ones can live in the ONE'S house, so all those 9 beans jump out of their house and join up with their new friend, Mr. Tenth bean! They all then jump into a snack size baggie (usable over and over) and go next door to live in the TEN'S house.

3. Repeat this process until you have ten baggies of beans trying to live in the TEN'S house. Of course only nine can live there, so all the baggies of ten jump into a bigger bag (you will only need one of these this year) and make the move to their new house, the HUNDRED'S house. You can also use buttons, paper clips, or basically any small item. They don't even have to be all the same kind of item.

4. Place Value Village tutorial video: https://www.youtube.com/watch?v=fuZ7Y3fDe7c

*Dried kidney beans are the best for this, as they are very sturdy.

Grading subjective assignments

Most often with math the grading is very objective. For example, 2 + 2 = 4, and no amount of individual expression changes this answer. However, there are times in this course when the answer may depend on a student's reflections of what he or she has learned on a particular day or in a week of assignments. In these subjective cases, the teacher can base a grade for these responses on several more objective measures. Does the student seem to understand the question and answer it as clearly as possible? Does the answer seem complete or does it fail to answer all aspects of the question? So a student may receive full credit if they seemed to meet all the assignment requirements, may get a passing grade if they meet some of the requirements, or may need to repeat the assignment if they didn't meet any of the requirements.

A – Student showed complete mastery of concepts with no errors.

B – Student showed mastery of concepts with minimal errors.

C – Student showed partial mastery of concepts. Review of some concepts is needed.

D – Student showed minimal understanding of concepts. Review is needed.

F – Student did not show understanding of concepts. Review is needed.

First Semester Suggested Daily Schedule

Date	Day	Assignment	Due Date	✓	Grade
		First Semester–First Quarter			
Week 1	Day 1	Read Lesson 1 • Pages 15-16 Complete Lesson 1 Exercise 1 • Page 17			
	Day 2	Complete Lesson 1 Exercise 2 • Pages 18-19			
	Day 3	Complete Lesson 1 Exercise 3 • Page 20			
	Day 4	Complete Lesson 1 Exercise 4 • Pages 21-22			
	Day 5	Complete Lesson 1 Exercise 5 **Review Time** • Pages 23-24			
Week 2	Day 6	Read Lesson 2 • Pages 25-26 Complete Lesson 2 Exercise 1 • Pages 27-28			
	Day 7	Complete Lesson 2 Exercise 2 • Pages 29-30			
	Day 8	Complete Lesson 2 Exercise 3 • Pages 31-32			
	Day 9	Complete Lesson 2 Exercise 4 • Pages 33-34			
	Day 10	Complete Lesson 2 Exercise 5 **Review Time** • Pages 35-36			
Week 3	Day 11	Read Lesson 3 • Pages 37-38 Complete Lesson 3 Exercise 1 • Pages 39-40			
	Day 12	Complete Lesson 3 Exercise 2 • Pages 41-42			
	Day 13	Complete Lesson 3 Exercise 3 • Pages 43-44			
	Day 14	Complete Lesson 3 Exercise 4 • Pages 45-46			
	Day 15	Complete Lesson 3 Exercise 5 **Review Time** • Pages 47-48			
Week 4	Day 16	Read Lesson 4 • Pages 49-50 Complete Lesson 4 Exercise 1 • Pages 51-52			
	Day 17	Complete Lesson 4 Exercise 2 • Pages 53-54			
	Day 18	Complete Lesson 4 Exercise 3 • Pages 55-56			
	Day 19	Complete Lesson 4 Exercise 4 • Pages 57-58			
	Day 20	Complete Lesson 4 Exercise 5 **Review Time** • Pages 59-60			
Week 5	Day 21	Read Lesson 5 • Pages 61-62 Complete Lesson 5 Exercise 1 • Page 63			
	Day 22	Complete Lesson 5 Exercise 2 • Pages 64-65			
	Day 23	Complete Lesson 5 Exercise 3 • Page 66 • Manipulatives • Page 335			
	Day 24	Complete Lesson 5 Exercise 4 • Page 67			
	Day 25	Complete Lesson 5 Exercise 5 **Review Time** • Pages 68-72			
Week 6	Day 26	Read Lesson 6 • Pages 73-74 Complete Lesson 6 Exercise 1 • Pages 75-76			
	Day 27	Complete Lesson 6 Exercise 2 • Pages 77-78			
	Day 28	Complete Lesson 6 Exercise 3 • Pages 79-80			
	Day 29	Complete Lesson 6 Exercise 4 • Pages 81-83			
	Day 30	Complete Lesson 6 Exercise 5 **Review Time** • Page 84			

Date	Day	Assignment	Due Date	✓	Grade
Week 7	Day 31	Read Lesson 7 • Page 85 Complete Lesson 7 Exercise 1 • Pages 86-88 Manipulatives • Pages 327-331			
	Day 32	Complete Lesson 7 Exercise 2 • Pages 89-90			
	Day 33	Complete Lesson 7 Exercise 3 • Pages 91-92			
	Day 34	Complete Lesson 7 Exercise 4-5 • Pages 93-94			
	Day 35	Math In Action Day: Point out math in cooking, doing laundry, watching television, and other relevant activities. Connect it with what your student has learned so far.			
Week 8	Day 36	Read Lesson 8 • Pages 95-96 Complete Lesson 8 Exercise 1 • Page 97			
	Day 37	Complete Lesson 8 Exercise 2 • Page 98			
	Day 38	Complete Lesson 8 Exercise 3 • Page 99			
	Day 39	Complete Lesson 8 Exercise 4 • Page 100 Manipulatives • Page 337			
	Day 40	Complete Lesson 8 Exercise 5 Show and Tell **Review** Pages 101-102			
Week 9	Day 41	Read Lesson 9 • Page 103 Complete Lesson 9 Exercise 1 **Review Week** • Page 104			
	Day 42	Complete Lesson 9 Exercise 2 **Review Week** • Pages 105-106			
	Day 43	Complete Lesson 9 Exercise 3 **Review Week** • Page 107			
	Day 44	Complete Lesson 9 Exercise 4 **Review Week** • Page 108			
	Day 45	Complete Lesson 9 Exercise 5 **Review Week** • Pages 109-110			
First Semester-Second Quarter					
Week 1	Day 46	Read Lesson 10 • Pages 111-112 Complete Lesson 10 Exercise 1 • Pages 113-114			
	Day 47	Complete Lesson 10 Exercise 2 • Page 115			
	Day 48	Complete Lesson 10 Exercise 3 • Page 116			
	Day 49	Complete Lesson 10 Exercise 4 • Page 117			
	Day 50	Complete Lesson 10 Exercise 5 **Review Time** • Page 118			
Week 2	Day 51	Read Lesson 11 • Page 119 Complete Lesson 11 Exercise 1 • Page 120			
	Day 52	Complete Lesson 11 Exercise 2 • Page 121			
	Day 53	Complete Lesson 11 Exercise 3 • Page 122			
	Day 54	Complete Lesson 11 Exercise 4 • Page 123			
	Day 55	Complete Lesson 11 Exercise 5 **Review Time** • Page 124			
Week 3	Day 56	Read Lesson 12 • Pages 125-126 Complete Lesson 12 Exercise 1 • Pages 127-128			
	Day 57	Complete Lesson 12 Exercise 2 • Pages 129-130			
	Day 58	Complete Lesson 12 Exercise 3 • Page 131			
	Day 59	Complete Lesson 12 Exercise 4 • Page 132 Manipulatives • Page 333			
	Day 60	Complete Lesson 12 Exercise 5 **Review Time** • Pages 133-134			

Date	Day	Assignment	Due Date	✓	Grade
Week 4	Day 61	Read Lesson 13 • Pages 135-136 Complete Lesson 13 Exercise 1 • Pages 137-138			
	Day 62	Complete Lesson 13 Exercise 2 • Page 139			
	Day 63	Complete Lesson 13 Exercise 3 • Pages 140-141			
	Day 64	Complete Lesson 13 Exercise 4 • Page 142			
	Day 65	Complete Lesson 13 Exercise 5 **Review Time** • Pages 143-144			
Week 5	Day 66	Read Lesson 14 • Page 145 Complete Lesson 14 Exercise 1 • Pages 146-147 Manipulatives • Page 339			
	Day 67	Complete Lesson 14 Exercise 2 • Page 148			
	Day 68	Complete Lesson 14 Exercise 3 • Page 149			
	Day 69	Complete Lesson 14 Exercise 4 • Page 150			
	Day 70	Complete Lesson 14 Exercise 5 **Review Time** • Pages 151-152			
Week 6	Day 71	Read Lesson 15 • Pages 153-154 Complete Lesson 15 Exercise 1 • Page 155 Manipulatives • Page 344			
	Day 72	Complete Lesson 15 Exercise 2 • Page 156			
	Day 73	Complete Lesson 15 Exercise 3 • Page 157			
	Day 74	Complete Lesson 15 Exercise 4 • Page 158			
	Day 75	Complete Lesson 15 Exercise 5 **Review Time** • Page 159-160			
Week 7	Day 76	Read Lesson 16 • Pages 161-162 Complete Lesson 16 Exercise 1 • Page 163-164			
	Day 77	Complete Lesson 16 Exercise 2 • Page 165			
	Day 78	Complete Lesson 16 Exercise 3 • Page 166			
	Day 79	Complete Lesson 16 Exercise 4 • Page 167			
	Day 80	Complete Lesson 16 Exercise 5 **Review Time** • Page 168			
Week 8	Day 81	Read Lesson 17 • Pages 169-172 Complete Lesson 17 Exercise 1 • Page 173			
	Day 82	Complete Lesson 17 Exercise • Page 174			
	Day 83	Complete Lesson 17 Exercise 3 • Pages 175-176			
	Day 84	Complete Lesson 17 Exercise 4 • Page 177			
	Day 85	Complete Lesson 17 Exercise 5 **Review Time** • Page 178			
Week 9	Day 86	Read Lesson 18 • Pages 179-180 Complete Lesson 18 Exercise 1 • Page 181			
	Day 87	Complete Lesson 18 Exercise 2 • Page 182			
	Day 88	Complete Lesson 18 Exercise 3 • Page 183			
	Day 89	Complete Lesson 18 Exercise 4 • Page 184			
	Day 90	Complete Lesson 18 Exercise 5 **Review Time** • Pages 185-186 Appendix • Page 343			
		Mid-Term Grade			

Second Semester Suggested Daily Schedule

Date	Day	Assignment	Due Date	✓	Grade
		Second Semester–Third Quarter			
Week 1	Day 91	Read Lesson 19 • Pages 187-188 Complete Lesson 19 Exercise 1 • Page 189			
	Day 92	Complete Lesson 19 Exercise 2 • Page 190			
	Day 93	Complete Lesson 19 Exercise 3 • Page 191			
	Day 94	Complete Lesson 19 Exercise 4 • Page 192			
	Day 95	Complete Lesson 19 Exercise 5 **Review Time** • Pages 193-194			
Week 2	Day 96	Read Lesson 20 • Page 195 Complete Lesson 20 Exercise 1 • Page 196			
	Day 97	Complete Lesson 20 Exercise 2 • Page 197			
	Day 98	Complete Lesson 20 Exercise 3 • Page 198			
	Day 99	Complete Lesson 20 Exercise 4 • Page 199			
	Day 100	Complete Lesson 20 Exercise 5 **Review Time** • Page 200			
Week 3	Day 101	Read Lesson 21 • Page 201 Complete Lesson 21 Exercise 1 • Page 202			
	Day 102	Complete Lesson 21 Exercise 2 • Page 203			
	Day 103	Complete Lesson 21 Exercise 3 • Page 204			
	Day 104	Complete Lesson 21 Exercise 4 • Page 205			
	Day 105	Complete Lesson 21 Exercise 5 **Review Time** • Page 206			
Week 4	Day 106	Read Lesson 22 • Pages 207-208 Complete Lesson 22 Exercise 1 • Page 209			
	Day 107	Complete Lesson 22 Exercise 2 • Page 210			
	Day 108	Complete Lesson 22 Exercise 3 • Page 211			
	Day 109	Complete Lesson 22 Exercise 4 • Page 212			
	Day 110	Complete Lesson 22 Exercise 5 **Review Time** • Pages 213-214			
Week 5	Day 111	Read Lesson 23 • Pages 215-216 Complete Lesson 23 Exercise 1 • Page 217			
	Day 112	Complete Lesson 23 Exercise 2 • Page 218			
	Day 113	Complete Lesson 23 Exercise 3 • Page 219			
	Day 114	Complete Lesson 23 Exercise 4 • Page 220			
	Day 115	Complete Lesson 23 Exercise 5 **Review Time** • Pages 221-222			
Week 6	Day 116	Read Lesson 24 • Pages 223-224 Complete Lesson 24 Exercise 1 • Page 225 Appendix • Page 341			
	Day 117	Complete Lesson 24 Exercise 2 • Page 226			
	Day 118	Complete Lesson 24 Exercise 3 • Page 227			
	Day 119	Complete Lesson 24 Exercise 4 • Page 228			
	Day 120	Complete Lesson 24 Exercise 5 **Review Time** • Pages 229-230			

Date	Day	Assignment	Due Date	✓	Grade
Week 7	Day 121	Read Lesson 25 • Pages 231-232 Complete Lesson 25 Exercise 1 • Pages 233-234			
	Day 122	Complete Lesson 25 Exercise 2 • Page 235			
	Day 123	Complete Lesson 25 Exercise 3 • Pages 236-237			
	Day 124	Complete Lesson 25 Exercise 4 • Page 238			
	Day 125	Complete Lesson 25 Exercise 5 **Review Time** • Pages 239-240			
Week 8	Day 126	Read Lesson 26 • Pages 241-242 Complete Lesson 26 Exercise 1 • Page 243			
	Day 127	Complete Lesson 26 Exercise 2 • Page 244			
	Day 128	Complete Lesson 26 Exercise 3 • Pages 245-246			
	Day 129	Complete Lesson 26 Exercise 4 • Pages 247-248			
	Day 130	Complete Lesson 26 Exercise 5 **Review Time** • Pages 249-250			
Week 9	Day 131	Read Lesson 27 • Page 251 Complete Lesson 27 Exercise 1 • Pages 252-253			
	Day 132	Complete Lesson 27 Exercise 2 • Page 254			
	Day 133	Complete Lesson 27 Exercise 3 • Page 255			
	Day 134	Complete Lesson 27 Exercise 4 • Page 256			
	Day 135	Complete Lesson 27 Exercise 5 **Review Time** • Pages 257-258			
		Second Semester-Fourth Quarter			
Week 1	Day 136	Read Lesson 28 • Page 259 Complete Lesson 28 Exercise 1 • Pages 260-261			
	Day 137	Complete Lesson 28 Exercise 2 • Page 262			
	Day 138	Complete Lesson 28 Exercise 3 • Pages 263-264			
	Day 139	Complete Lesson 28 Exercise 4 • Page 265			
	Day 140	Complete Lesson 28 Exercise 5 **Review Time** • Page 266			
Week 2	Day 141	Read Lesson 29 • Pages 267-268 Complete Lesson 29 Exercise 1 • Page 269			
	Day 142	Complete Lesson 29 Exercise 2 • Page 270			
	Day 143	Complete Lesson 29 Exercise 3 • Pages 271-272			
	Day 144	Complete Lesson 29 Exercise 4 • Page 273			
	Day 145	Complete Lesson 29 Exercise 5 **Review Time** • Page 274			
Week 3	Day 146	Read Lesson 30 • Pages 275-276 Complete Lesson 30 Exercise 1 • Page 277			
	Day 147	Complete Lesson 30 Exercise 2 • Page 278			
	Day 148	Complete Lesson 30 Exercise 3 • Page 279			
	Day 149	Complete Lesson 30 Exercise 4 • Page 280			
	Day 150	Complete Lesson 30 Exercise 5 **Review Time** • Pages 281-282			
Week 4	Day 151	Read Lesson 31 • Page 283 Complete Lesson 31 Exercise 1• Pages 284-285			
	Day 152	Complete Lesson 31 Exercise 2 • Pages 286-287			
	Day 153	Complete Lesson 31 Exercise 3 • Pages 288-289			
	Day 154	Complete Lesson 31 Exercise 4 • Pages 290-291			
	Day 155	Complete Lesson 31 Exercise 5 **Review Time** • Page 292			

Date	Day	Assignment	Due Date	✓	Grade
Week 5	Day 156	Read Lesson 32 • Page 293 Complete Lesson 32 Exercise 1 • Page 294			
	Day 157	Complete Lesson 32 Exercise 2 • Page 295			
	Day 158	Complete Lesson 32 Exercise 3 • Page 296			
	Day 159	Complete Lesson 32 Exercise 4 • Page 297			
	Day 160	Complete Lesson 32 Exercise 5 **Review Time** • Page 298			
Week 6	Day 161	Read Lesson 33 • Page 299 Complete Lesson 33 Exercise 1 • Page 300			
	Day 162	Complete Lesson 33 Exercise 2 • Page 301			
	Day 163	Complete Lesson 33 Exercise 3 • Page 302			
	Day 164	Complete Lesson 33 Exercise 4 • Page 303			
	Day 165	Complete Lesson 33 Exercise 5 **Review Time** • Page 304			
Week 7	Day 166	Read Lesson 34 • Page 305 Complete Lesson 34 Exercise 1 • Page 306			
	Day 167	Complete Lesson 34 Exercise 2 • Page 307			
	Day 168	Complete Lesson 34 Exercise 3 • Page 308			
	Day 169	Complete Lesson 34 Exercise 4 – 5 • Pages 309-310			
	Day 170	Number Hunt! Have the student find examples of items that number from 1 to 20 in your classroom or home.			
Week 8	Day 171	Read Lesson 35 • Page 311 Complete Lesson 35 Exercise 1 • Page 312			
	Day 172	Complete Lesson 35 Exercise 2 • Pages 313-314			
	Day 173	Complete Lesson 35 Exercise 3 • Page 315			
	Day 174	Complete Lesson 35 Exercise 4 • Page 316			
	Day 175	Complete Lesson 35 Exercise 5 **Review Time** • Pages 317-318			
Week 9	Day 176	Read Lesson 36 • Page 319 Complete Lesson 36 Exercise 1 • Page 320			
	Day 177	Complete Lesson 36 Exercise 2 • Page 321			
	Day 178	Complete Lesson 36 Exercise 3 • Page 322			
	Day 179	Complete Lesson 36 Exercise 4 • Page 323			
	Day 180	Complete Lesson 36 Exercise 5 • Page 324			
		Final Grade			

The Adventure Begins!
We Learn Numbers 0–9

Welcome to a wonderful adventure! We are going to have so much fun learning together this year. Do you know that there are numbers, patterns, and shapes all around us? This is the story of Charlie and Charlotte. They are brother and sister twins, who have come to spend the summer at their grandparents' farm. This is Charlie and Charlotte and their pet turtle, Pokey.

When they arrived at the farm this morning, the twins were a little sad to see their Mom and Dad leave, but they knew they would talk with them soon via videocall. Grandpa and Grandma were so excited to have them here on their farm! They told them about all of the new baby animals that were born this spring. The children can't wait to visit the barn and see all of them. Grandpa said they can go right after lunch, and then they are going to help him in the smaller of the two gardens.

The farm was beautiful! With the big red barn and white farmhouse, it looked like a picture in a storybook. Grandma's flowers nodded their heads at them as if they were saying, "Hello!" Pokey seemed to feel right at home, because he started eating grass and exploring Grandma's rock garden.

Grandpa and Grandma are very organized, and their farm is very orderly. The twins noticed that Grandpa used numbers to organize almost everything on his farm. From the stalls in the barn to the rows of vegetables in the garden, everything had numbers. The twins thought this was interesting, so they asked Grandpa

why he did this. Grandpa chuckled and said, "I organize my animals in the barn and my vegetables in the kitchen garden by using numbers because it helps me to be more productive. I often use the numbers that I'm sure you two already have seen…look, here are the numbers or numerals, 0, 1, 2, 3, 4, 5, 6, 7, 8, and 9."

The twins looked at each other and nodded, " Yes, Grandpa, Mom taught us those numbers already. We know that the number 0 means nothing. Is that why you have it on this row - because nothing is planted here?" Grandpa nodded and smiled.

"Yes, I left that row empty - with 0 plants - because I thought you two would like to plant something there." The twins nodded and smiled. They would indeed like to plant something in Grandpa's garden!

Grandpa walked to the next row and said, "There are nine more rows of vegetables in my garden. Row 1 has only 1 plant in it! Look, this is a giant pumpkin, and it will take all the room up all by itself! Next, we have row 2. Row 2 has 2 plants in it." Grandpa held up two fingers to show what two looks like. "These two plants are zucchini plants. They also need a lot of room, because they grow really long vines. Row 3 has three sweet potato plants in it, and row 4 has 4 tomato plants inside these funny, round cages. Row 5 has 5 green bean plants, row 6 has 6 sugar snap plants growing on a fence, row 7 has 7 beets, row 8 has 8 corn plants, and row 9 has 9 carrot plants. Do you understand now?" They both nodded.

Later that evening, Charlie and Charlotte knelt by the coffee table while Grandma read a bedtime story. They wanted to practice writing the numbers or numerals Grandpa had shown them earlier. Why don't you practice too?

Trace the numbers below.

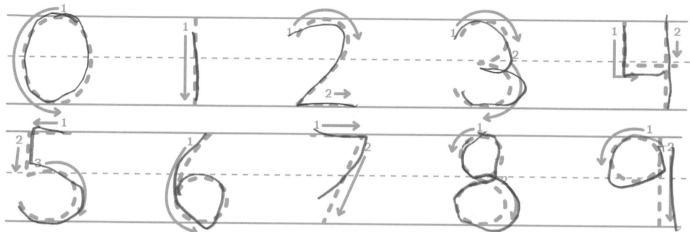

Remember, each of the numbers stands for a certain amount of something. Trace the numbers again, copy them on the lines below, then draw that many dots next to each number. Number 5 is done for you.

Let's try something new! Charlie and Charlotte discovered numbers in their Grandpa's garden and barn. See if you can discover numbers around your house. Draw pictures of what you find next to the correct number below. Count the objects you drew to make sure you have the right amount.

1 _____

2 _____

3 _____

4 _____

5 _____

6 _____

7 _____

8 _____

9 _____

On the next page, trace the numbers and match them to the group of turtles showing the correct amount. Number 1 is done for you.

(Remember! "0" means "nothing.")

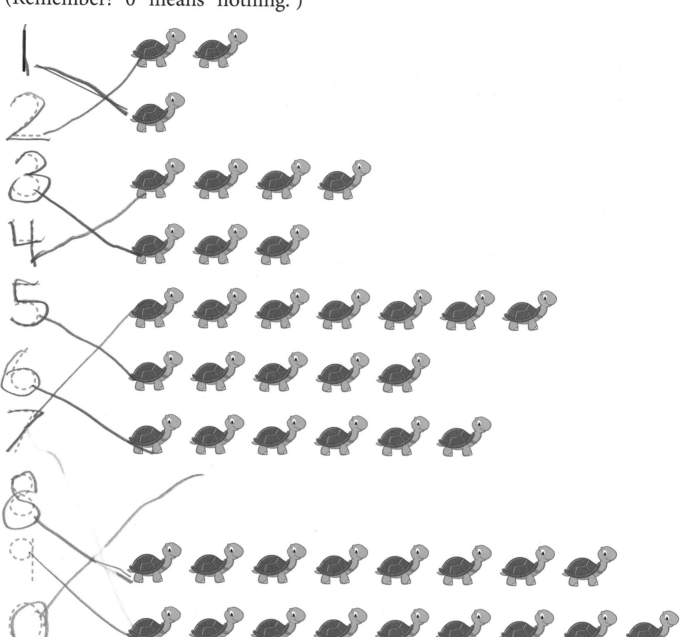

How old are you? Write the number that shows your age. ___6___

How many fingers do you have on each hand? ___5___

How many eyes do you have? ___2___

How many legs do you have? ___2___

Here are the numbers you have learned so far. Trace them with your finger as you say them out loud. Then practice writing the numbers you have learned. Say them as you write them.

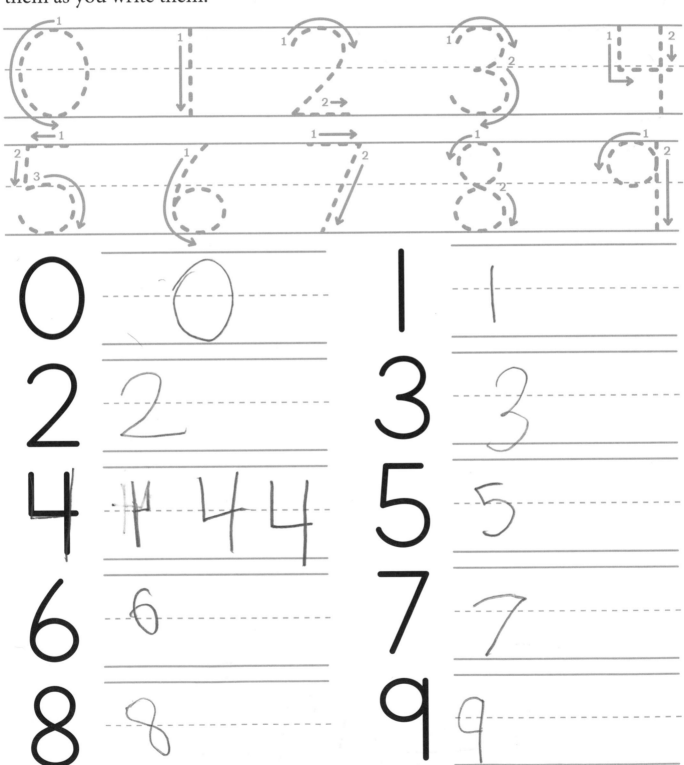

The next morning, after breakfast, Charlie and Charlotte ran to the barn to visit the baby animals. It was a beautiful sunny day, with a sky the color of a robin egg.

"Charlie, let's practice counting the baby animals!" Charlotte said excitedly.

"Okay, Charlotte, let's start with the baby pigs! Grandpa said that baby pigs are called piglets. Aren't they cute?" Charlie answered. The twins knelt to look through the gate.

How many piglets does this mommy pig have? ___6___

Next they counted the puppies.

How many puppies did the farm dog have this spring? ___7___

Now it's your turn! Write the number showing how many babies of each kind of animal was born on the farm. The first one is done for you.

There are <u>6</u> baby chickens (chicks).

There are __7__ baby cats (kittens).

There are __2__ baby goats (kids).

There are __3__ baby rabbits (bunnies).

There is __1__ baby horse (foal).

There are __4__ baby cows (calves).

There are __9__ baby ducks (ducklings).

There are __5__ baby sheep (lambs).

Review Time!

Help the twins write their letter.

After an exciting morning of playing with the baby farm animals and helping Grandpa in the barn, the twins ate a picnic lunch of peanut butter and strawberry jam sandwiches made with Grandma's fresh homemade bread. Delicious! "Why don't you two go in and sit down at the kitchen table and write your parents a letter?" Grandma said, "I'm sure they would love to hear all about your visit so far."

"Yes, that sounds like fun!" the children said excitedly.

Dear Mom and Dad,

   We are having so much fun with Grandpa and Grandma! Grandpa showed us these numbers! (You can look back in your lesson if you need to!)

___0___ , ___1___ , ___2___ , ___3___ , ___4___ ,

___5___ , ___6___ , ___7___ , ___8___ , ___9___

And this is what they mean! (Match them.)

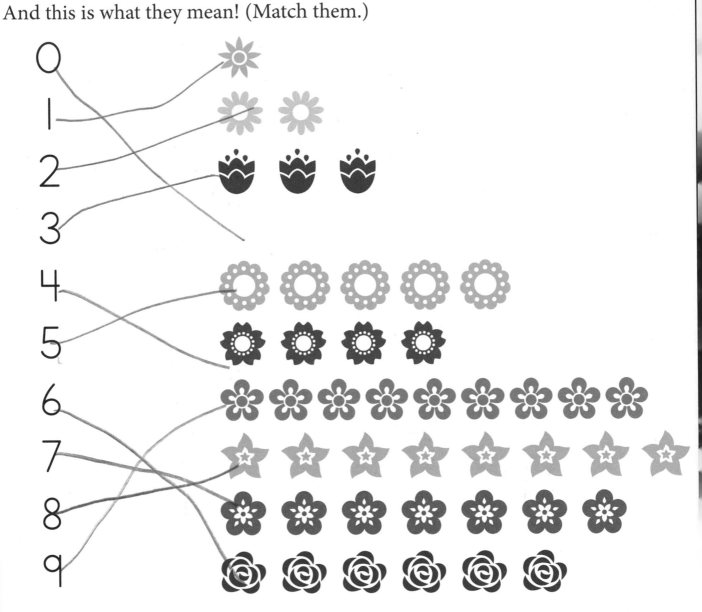

We love you!

P.S. Did you know there are numbers all around us?

How Many Eggs? Review of Numbers 0 – 9

"Children, I have something very special that I need help with today," Grandma told the twins the next morning, while they helped her wash the breakfast dishes.

"What is it, Grandma?" they asked together. "I need to finish preparing my egg orders this morning," Grandma explained. "I have customers who live in town and can't keep chickens. They come here to our farm every Tuesday afternoon to pick up their eggs for the week. Grandpa goes out early every morning and gathers all the eggs for me. I need your help finishing up the washing and sorting. Do you think you can help? We have to count the eggs and make sure each order has the right number of cartons in it."

"We can do it, Grandma! We know our numbers now. We want to help!" the twins jumped up and down excitedly.

"Ok, but we have to be very careful! Eggs are extremely fragile, which means it is very easy to break them," Grandma told the children. "These are the dirty eggs. We will wash them with a warm, wet rag first. Then we will place them in these cartons. Six eggs go in each carton. I will tell you how!"

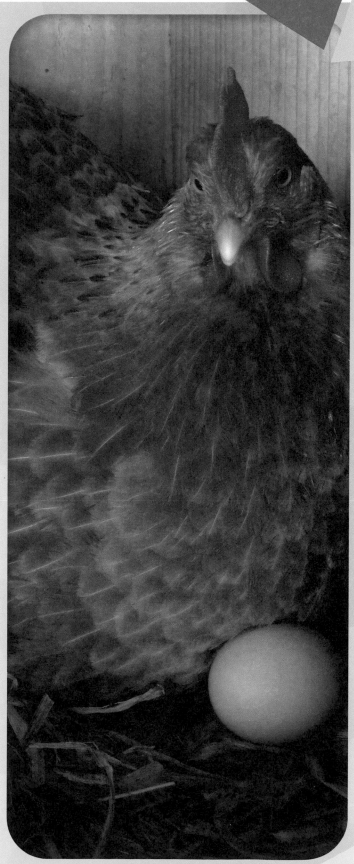

The children nodded their heads and followed Grandma's instructions carefully. It was hard work washing the eggs carefully and placing them in the cartons. While they worked, Grandma told them a story of when she was a little girl living on her parents' farm. It had been her job to take care of the chickens and gather the eggs. That was a long time ago, and the twins giggled imagining Grandma as a little girl!

Charlie and Charlotte liked the feel of the warm, brown eggs. They had never seen brown eggs before. They were used to the white eggs that Mommy and Daddy bought at the grocery store near their home in town.

After they had finished washing the eggs and placing them in cartons, Grandma gave them cards with her customers' names written on them. Next to their names, were numbers, showing how many cartons of eggs each customer wanted.

Can you help Charlie and Charlotte match the name and number cards with the correct customer order of eggs? The first one is done for you.

Smiths 3

Jones 7

Browns 9

Davises 4

Mrs. Sanders 1

Mr. Winkle 2

Rev. Joe 5

Carlsons 8

Halls 6

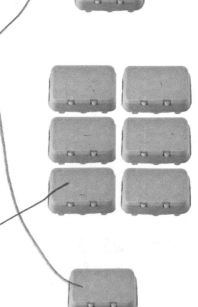

After the twins finished helping Grandma with her egg orders, they decided to practice writing their numbers again. This is a good chance to practice your numbers also.

On these lines fill in the missing numerals:

_0_ , 1, 2, _3_ , 4, _5_ , _6_ , 7,

_8_ , _9_

On these lines, write all the numbers we have learned from 0-9.

_0_ , _1_ , _2_ , _3_ , _4_ ,

_5_ , _6_ , _7_ , _8_ , _9_

Remember, numbers stand for a certain amount of something.
Draw a line under the correct number of flowers. The first one is done
for you.

2   ✿ ✿ ✿ ✿ ✿
    ____

4   ✿ ✿ ✿ ✿ ✿ ✿
    _____

7   ✿ ✿ ✿ ✿ ✿ ✿ ✿ ✿ ✿
    _____

1   ✿ ✿ ✿ ✿
    __

5   ✿ ✿ ✿ ✿ ✿ ✿ ✿ ✿
    _____

9   ✿ ✿ ✿ ✿ ✿ ✿ ✿ ✿ ✿ ✿

3   ✿ ✿ ✿ ✿ ✿ ✿
    ____

6   ✿ ✿ ✿ ✿ ✿ ✿ ✿ ✿ ✿
    _____

8   ✿ ✿ ✿ ✿ ✿ ✿ ✿ ✿ ✿ ✿ ✿ ✿
    _____

Color in the right number of eggs.

5

3

6

2

8

9

0

1

4

7

Name_____

Charlie and Charlotte have discovered numbers all around them!
How about you? Can you count the objects and write the correct number?

      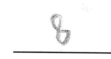

_____ 7 _____   _____ 8 _____   _____ a _____

_____ 4 _____   _____ 8 _____   _____ 3 _____

_____ 7 _____   _____ 2 _____   _____ 1 _____

How about counting things you have and do? Try it!

How many plates do you eat on at supper? _____ 1 _____

How many snacks do you eat in a day? _____ 5 _____

How many shoes are you wearing? _____ 2 _____

How many clocks are in your kitchen? _____ 1 _____

Numbers for copywork. Copy and say these numbers.

Let's do it again!

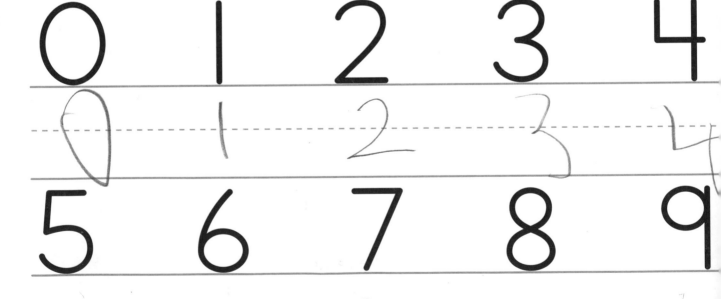

Can you say all the numbers we have learned, without looking at them?

"Thank you, children, for helping with the egg orders," Grandma hugged the twins close. "It is so nice to have such wonderful grandchildren! I love you so much."

"We love you, too, Grandma!" the twins exclaimed then added, "Grandma, could you tell us about chickens? How are baby chickens born?"

Grandma chuckled. "Oh, that is an amazing subject! Come here, children, I'll tell you all about the miracle of a chicken's life." She took a piece of paper out of the desk drawer and invited the twins to sit with her at the table. They watched as she sketched something on the paper.

"This is the egg. We washed a lot of eggs this morning, didn't we? Those eggs are the ones that we take to eat and sell, but there are certain eggs that have babies (chicks) in them! The ones that have the chicks in them are kept warm for twenty-one days-that's three whole weeks!"

"God made chickens in an amazing way!" Grandma took the children's hands in hers and held them to her heart. "Do you feel that?" The children nodded their heads. "That is my heart beating. Here, feel yours now." She placed their hands on their chests where they could feel their hearts beating. "Do you know that a baby chicken has a heart too?" Grandma asked. "In fact, their heart is beating quite a while before they come out of their eggs."

Charlie's and Charlotte's eyes grew round. "Really, Grandma? Please tell us more!" Grandma smiled and drew something else on the paper.

"This is the baby chick inside of an egg. Do you see this funny little space at the top of the egg?

That little space is very special. You see, when God created chicks, He gave them a special little sack to grow in, inside of the egg. That sack is smaller than the egg shell, which leaves this little space at the top. After exactly twenty-one days, the chick starts pecking its way out of the shell. It pecks its way into that special space. When it gets through the sack and into that space, it can get more air, making it able to keep pecking through the shell!"

Charlie's eyes were round. "But Grandma, how does the baby chick know when to come out?" he asked.

"That is a very good question, Charlie. God puts something like a little alarm clock inside of each chick which tells it exactly when to come out. Some people call it instinct. I believe that it's just another little way of God showing us how awesome He is. It also shows that God is a God of order, and that He uses patterns and numbers too!" Grandma smiled and patted the children's heads. "Why don't you two take a few minutes and write your parents a letter before your bath time. I'm sure they would love to hear everything you have been learning!"

Review Time!

Help the children write their parents a letter telling what they have learned. You can show what you have learned also.

Dear Mom and Dad,

Guess what? We got to help Grandma with her egg orders today! We washed the eggs in warm water and put them in cartons for her. Then we counted and sorted the cartons for each of the customers. We are getting really good at counting! Look what else we have learned about numbers:

Write the number that comes before. | Write the number that comes after.

4, 5

8, 9

2, 3

0, 1

2, 7

6, 5

4, 3

8, 7

2, 1

0, ___

Grandma told us about how baby chickens are born! It's really amazing!

We drew a picture for you:

 (Draw a picture of a chick in an egg.)

Love, Charlie, Charlotte and our friend, _____

Are you having a good time with Charlie and Charlotte at their grandparents' farm? We have been learning a lot! Isn't it fun to play and learn together? So far we have learned and reviewed about numbers 0–9, and today we are going to learn about something new.

Did you know that there are shapes all around us? A shape is another way to say the "form" of something. If you look at the front of this book when it is closed, you can see that its form or shape has 4 corners. It also has four sides. Take a look at the book right now and count the corners and sides.

Write how many corners here: _____.

Write how many sides here: _____.

The shape of this book is called a **rectangle**. A rectangle has 4 corners, which are called <u>right angles</u>. You saw that this book also has 4 sides. Did you see that 2 of the sides are longer and 2 are shorter? That is exactly what makes a rectangle. This is what a rectangle looks like.

You can see that it doesn't matter which way the rectangle is turned, it still has 2 shorter sides, 2 longer sides, and 4 corners, which are right angles.

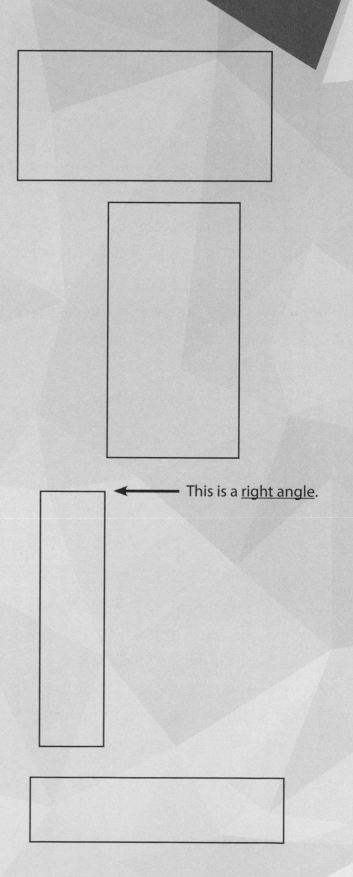

This is a <u>right angle</u>.

While Charlie and Charlotte were visiting their grandparents' farm, their pet turtle, Pokey, needed a bed to sleep in. The didn't want him to wander off at night and get lost in the house. Grandpa came to the rescue when he said, "I have just the right box in the attic! It will make the perfect bed for him. It is a rectangle, so there will be plenty of room to put his pillow in it."

The twins agreed. Mom had taught them about rectangles when they were younger, so they knew that a rectangle has four sides - two long sides and two shorter sides. They also knew that rectangles had four corners that looked like this:

"Yes, Grandpa! This box shaped like a rectangle is the perfect bed for Pokey." The children knelt on the floor to examine the box. "Let's put his pillow into it, so he knows that it is his bed." They ran to get the pillow and the sleepy turtle. Pokey liked his new and bed, and Grandpa was right - Pokey's pillow fit perfectly into the rectangle-shaped box.

Color each rectangle with a red crayon. Remember, rectangles have 2 shorter sides, 2 longer sides, and 4 corners that look like this:

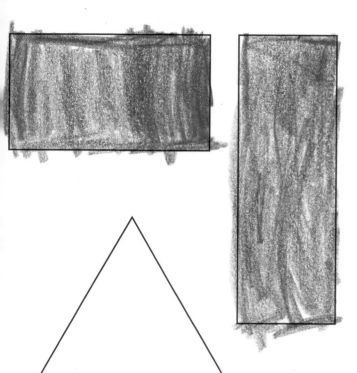

How many rectangles did you color? Write the number here:

4

Next to each group of rectangles, write the correct number.

 ___5___

 ___2___

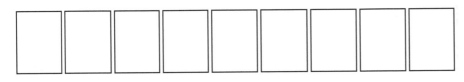 ___4___

 ___3___

 ___6___

 ___2___

 ___1___

 ___4___

 ___8___

Charlie and Charlotte are going to go on a rectangle hunt, and they want you to go too! In the space below, draw pictures of what you found on your rectangle hunt. Show your teacher, and then explain why they are rectangles.

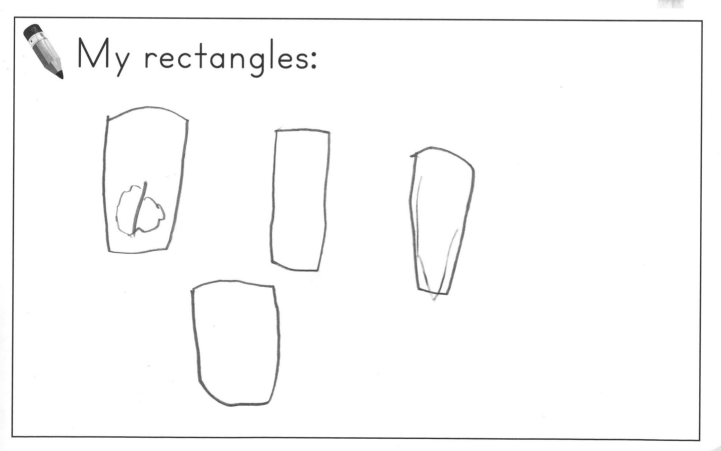

My rectangles:

Name________________________________

Numbers for copywork. Copy the numbers and say them out loud.

0

1

2

3

4

5

6

7

8

9

Color the rectangles.

How many rectangles? _____

Name________________________________

Exercise 3

Day 13

Draw a rectangle around the correct number of objects. The first one is done for you.

8 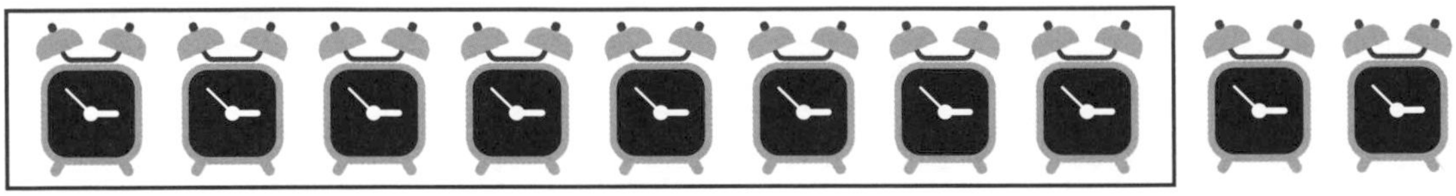

2 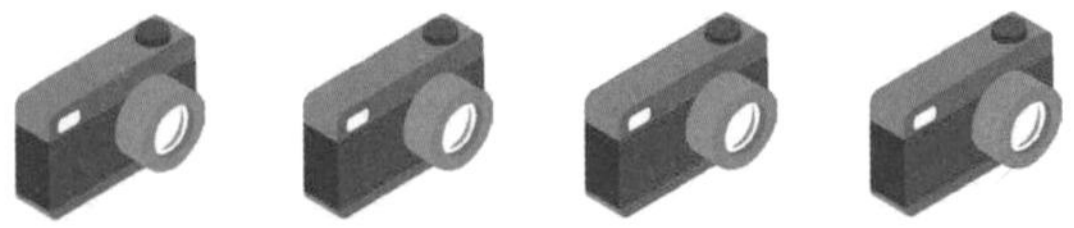

4 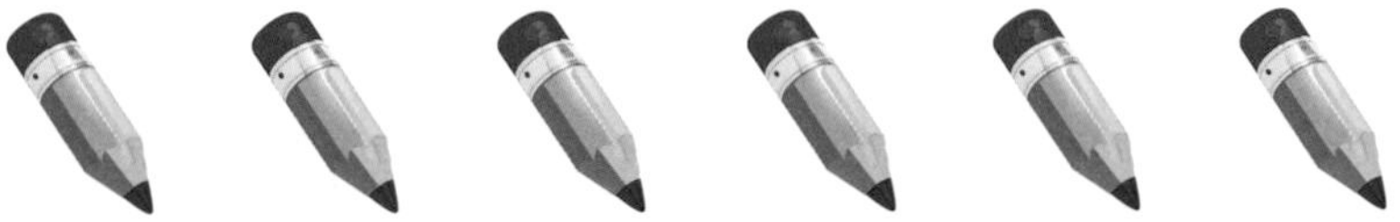

6 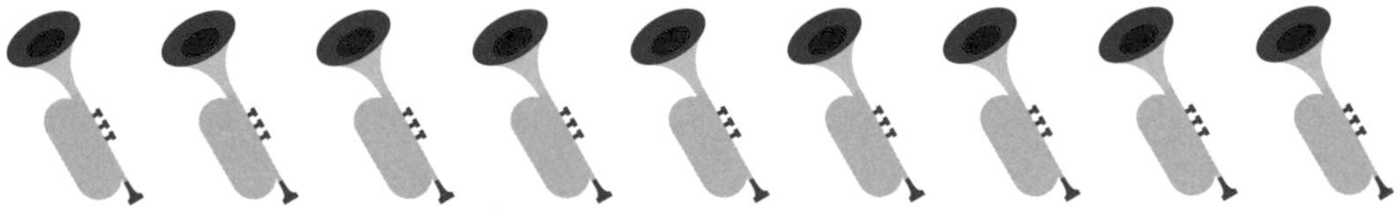

1 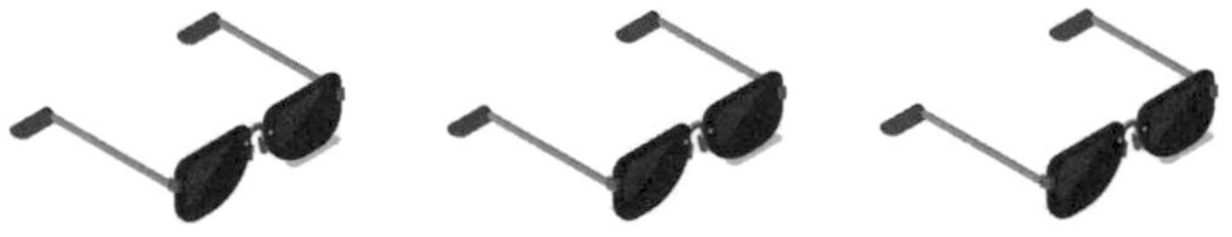

3 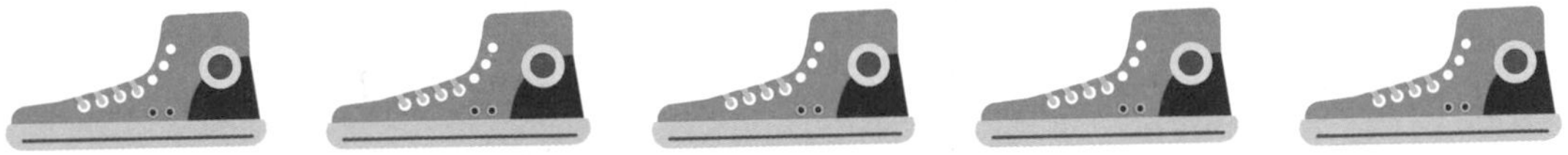

5 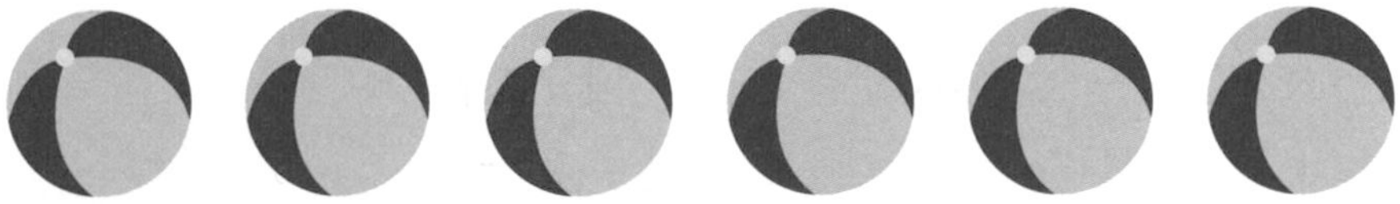

How many legs do turtles have? _____

How many eyes? _____

How many tails? _____

How many sides does a rectangle have? _____

How many corners does a rectangle have? _____

How many long sides does a rectangle have? _____

How many short sides does a rectangle have? _____

Meet Pokey

Pokey is a box turtle, which is one of the most common types of pet turtles. Charlie and Charlotte got Pokey as a gift for Christmas last year and they love him very much.

Turtles are extremely interesting creatures. God gave them something very special: a home they carry on their backs! Would you like to carry around your home on your back?

Turtles are in the reptile family. Reptile babies hatch from eggs like baby chickens do, but reptile babies do not have feathers. They have scales or shells.

Turtles are truly amazing creatures!

Name________________________________

Exercise 4

Day 14

Numbers for copywork. Copy the numbers and say them.

0 ____________

1 ____________

2 ____________

3 ____________

4 ____________

5 ____________

6 ____________

7 ____________

8 ____________

9 ____________

Review Time!

Review what we have learned so far. Fill in the missing numbers and trace the others:

Let's do it again!

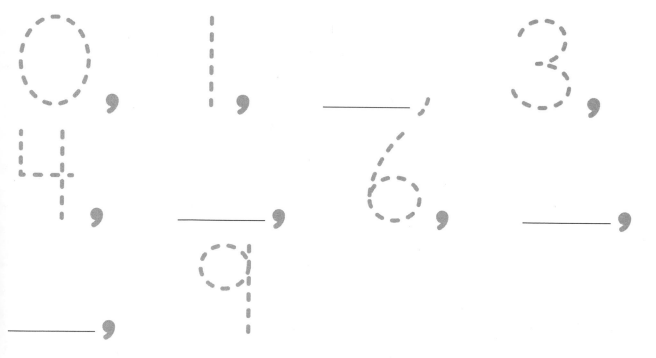

Color all the rectangles blue.

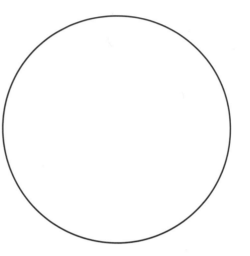
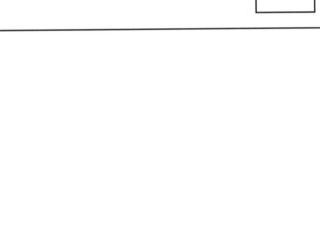
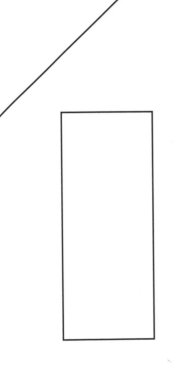
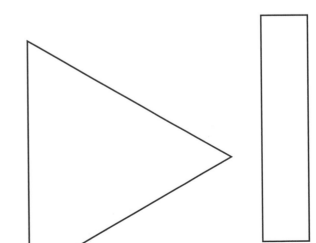

Circles and Patterns

The twins were excited to learn more about rectangles! They realized that there were rectangles all around them on the farm. Charlotte discovered the kitchen table was a rectangle when she helped Grandma set the table for supper.

As they sat together that evening, enjoying Grandma's delicious meal of roast beef, mashed potatoes, and fresh carrots, Grandpa said, "Charlie and Charlotte, did you know that there are many, many shapes? Look at our dinner plates. Do you know what this shape is called?"

The twins looked at each other. Neither one of them could remember what Mom had told them this shape was called. "Can you remind me, Grandpa," Charlotte replied. She knew that it was not a rectangle! Rectangles have 4 sides; 2 of them are shorter than the other 2. Rectangles also have 4 corners, which are right angles. Charlotte knew that rectangles look like this:

She knew the dinner plates did not look like that! They looked like this:

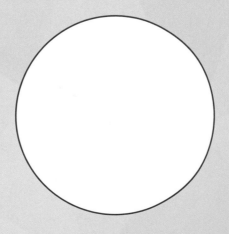

The twins could not remember the name for this shape, so Grandpa explained, "This shape is called a circle. A circle does not have corners. It does not have a beginning or end. Circles are my favorite shape because they remind me of my wedding ring! Look," said Grandpa as he held up his hand, "my wedding ring is a symbol of how much I love your grandma. Our love has no end just like this ring. I have had this ring for over 40 years, and I hope to have it for a long time to come!"

Grandma added, "Children, circles are very special shapes! Not just because they look like our wedding rings, but because they are a symbol of God's love for us. God is called the Alpha and Omega, which means 'the Beginning and the End.' His love for us goes on and on forever. Soon I will tell you just HOW much He loves us!"

Charlie and Charlotte's eyes were serious, and they nodded their heads. "We understand, Grandma and Grandpa. Mommy and Daddy always say that they love us forever and ever. Their love is like a circle too, isn't it?" asked Charlie.

"Yes, Charlie! Our whole family is like a circle. We love each other with a love that never ends," Grandma answered.

"I miss Mommy and Daddy," Charlotte whispered in a sad voice.

"Would you like to make them a picture? You could draw pictures, and I can help you write a letter," Grandma offered.

Both of the children nodded their heads. "I can draw a picture of the bed Grandpa made for Pokey," Charlie said.

"Yes! And I will draw them a circle!" Charlotte felt better thinking about her letter to her parents. While Charlie and Charlotte gather their art materials, we can practice some of the things we have learned together. After that, we will help the twins with their letters to their parents.

Name_____

Color all the rectangles red.

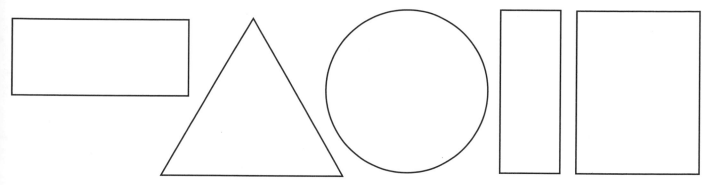

There are _____ rectangles colored red.

Color all the circles blue.

There are _____ circles colored blue.

Name____________________________

Exercise 1

Day 16

Numbers for copywork. Copy the numbers and say them.

0	5
1	6
2	7
3	8
4	9

Tell your teacher what makes a circle and what makes a rectangle. Find some circles around you.

 My circles:

Fill in the missing numbers and trace the others:

_____ , 1 , 2 , _____ ,

4 , _____ , _____ , 7 ,

_____ , _____

Let's do it again!

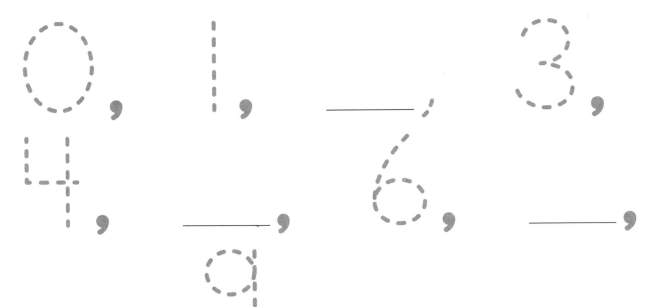

0 , 1 , _____ , 3 ,

4 , _____ , 6 , _____ ,

9

_____ ,

Now help Charlie write his letter!

Dear Mom and Dad,

Grandpa helped us make a bed for Pokey! It is a rectangle. Here is a picture of it. (Help Charlie by drawing a picture of Pokey's bed.)

Look what I can do! I can write all of my numbers! (Help Charlie write the numbers. Try to write them from memory.)

Also, did you know that turtles are hatched from eggs? Grandpa told us about reptiles! Pokey is a reptile! Here is my picture of a baby turtle coming out of its egg. (Help Charlie draw his picture of a turtle hatching.)

Love lots! Charlie

Let's practice what we have learned so far!

Draw a circle around each group of items. Count the items and write the correct number showing how many items are in each group.

_____   _____   _____

_____   _____   _____

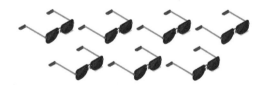

_____   _____   _____

What comes next? Color all the circles red and all the rectangles blue.

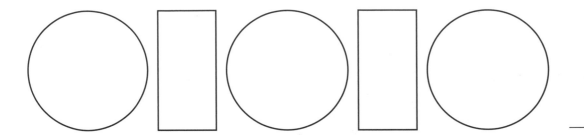

What you just colored is called a pattern. Let's try another pattern!

Draw a circle around what comes next.

 My pattern:

Review Time! Let's help Charlotte write her letter to her parents.

Dear Mom and Dad,

Today Grandpa taught us more about circles. I love circles! They are my favorite shape. Grandma said that they remind her of our family's love for each other, because they don't have an end. This is a circle. (Draw a circle for Charlotte's parents.)

I also learned about patterns. Did you know that there are patterns all around us? I made you this pattern, and my friends are going to help me finish it for you! (Circle the one that completes the pattern.)

  _____

I have been practicing my numbers and shapes! Look what I can do! (Write all the numbers we have learned. Try not to look back at the other lessons.)

I am getting really good at drawing rectangles also! I drew this rectangle for you. (Finish the rectangle for Charlotte's parents.)

Love, Charlotte

Bright and early the next morning, Charlie and Charlotte were helping Grandpa in his garden. The twins excitedly chattered about the new day stretching out in front of them. Grandpa smiled and nodded as they talked.

"Grandpa, Charlie and I have learned a lot since we came here!" Charlotte exclaimed.

"We sure have!" Charlie said letting out a high whistle. He was proud of his new skill, and he practiced it whenever he was outside. "Grandpa, have you ever noticed how many rectangles and circles are around us?" Charlie asked.

"Yes, Charlie, I have," Grandpa replied as he brushed the dirt off of his knees.

"Like that," Charlotte added, pointing to the big, red barn, "Grandpa's barn has lots and lots of rectangles. Look, the doors look like two big rectangles!"

Charlie turned and gazed at the barn. He loved the barn and spent as much time there as he could, swinging on the rope tied to the rafters. He nodded in agreement, "Yes, I see it too, Charlotte! And the silo is round like a circle. Grandpa, why do we notice more shapes around us than we use to?"

Grandpa chuckled, "That's because when we learn something new, we tend to think about it a lot. When we think about something, we notice it more. I'm thinking about breakfast right now! Shall we go in and see if Grandma has our breakfast ready for us?"

Charlotte giggled, "Yes! My tummy is making funny noises, and I can smell Grandma's blueberry pancakes from here!"

"And I can smell sausage!" Charlie added.

"Let's take these carrots in for Grandma, shall we?" Grandpa showed the children how to wash the vegetables off with the garden hose. "These will be delicious in Grandma's chicken vegetable soup!" The children laughed, "Grandpa, you are thinking about food a lot right now!"

"I suppose I am!" Grandpa laughed along with the children.

Color the rectangles green and the circles yellow.

Name______________________________

Trace the number you have learned with your finger and say them out loud.

0 5

1 6

2 7

3 8

4 9

Match the numbers with the correct group of objects.

6

5

3

7

1

9

4

2

8

Count the objects and write the correct number.

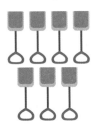      

_____   _____   _____

_____   _____   _____

_____   _____   _____

Using the number cards provided in the back of this book, put the numbers 0–9 in order after cutting them out. (You can store the cut-out numbers in a plastic bag.

Finish the picture by adding to the shapes! Add flowers and birds. Have fun!

After the children and Grandpa had washed their hands, Grandma gave each of them a plate of steaming blueberry pancakes, smothered in butter and maple syrup. They were so delicious!

"Grandma, where did you get these blueberries?" Charlie asked between bites, "I've never tasted such yummy little blueberries before! And why are they so tiny?"

Grandma grinned at Charlie. "These are from my secret blueberry patch, Charlie, and they are tiny because they are wild blueberries. Wild blueberries are a lot smaller and tastier than the type that are grown domestically, which means those that are planted by people."

"Will you show us where your secret blueberry patch is, Grandma?" Charlotte wanted to know.

"Then it wouldn't be a secret, would it?" teased Grandma with twinkling eyes. "Grandpa has been trying to get me to tell him about my blueberry patch for over ten years! But I won't tell him, because he might go and pick them when I am not watching!" Grandma pinched Grandpa's cheek affectionately, "He loves blueberries so much!"

Charlie was puzzled about something, so he asked, "Grandma, do blueberries grow under the ground?"

"No, Charlie, why would you ask that?" Grandma looked puzzled now too.

"Well, Grandpa has veggies in his garden that grow under the ground," Charlie said. "The carrots he brought in for you were covered in dirt because he pulled them out of the ground!"

Charlotte nodded and said, "Yes! I didn't even know they were there until Grandpa got a pitchfork and carefully lifted the dirt next to the carrot plant! All of the sudden, I saw the carrots! Why do they grow under the ground, Grandpa?"

Grandma smiled, "You children are very curious, aren't you! I'm so glad you are, because that is how you learn!"

Grandpa reached over and picked up one of the carrots off of the counter. He held it up for the children to see, "On a carrot, we eat the roots of the plant. We call it a root vegetable because of this. There are other root vegetables too, like the potatoes Grandma made last night. Those also grow under the ground! Green beans grow on top of the ground, on the bean plants. We can go along and pick them off of the plant from the top, but root vegetables have to be pulled up."

Carrots grow under the ground. To eat them, we have to pull or dig them out.

This is a wild blueberry bush. Blueberries do not grow under the ground like carrots.

The children looked at each other with round eyes. They were amazed! "Grandma, can we draw a picture of this for Mommy and Daddy?" Charlie asked.

"May you draw it," Grandma corrected with a twinkle in her eye, "and, yes, you may! But please help clear the breakfast table first."

Help the twins draw a picture of what you have learned about root veggies.

Review Time!

On the line below, write the numbers we have learned so far:

_____

- -

_____

_____

- -

_____

Explain to your teacher what a rectangle is. Draw one here:

Explain to your teacher what a circle is. Draw one here:

Next to each number, draw shapes to show how many.

2 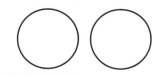 Example

5

6

9

0

1

3

7

4

8

In the space below, draw a pattern using shapes that we have learned.

More Numbers, Patterns, Shapes; Introducing Triangles

The twins had been at Grandma and Grandpa's farm for almost a week. They were having a lot of fun learning about the different kinds of vegetables in the garden, and they loved helping Grandpa feed the animals.

It seemed like they were learning something new every day! They were now good helpers, because they were used to being around the animals. They also liked helping Grandma in her kitchen. She was always baking or cooking something that smelled wonderful, and they were always there to taste-test the recipe.

One morning after the breakfast dishes were dried and put away, Charlotte and Charlie asked Grandma if they could go exploring. They wanted to go down to the pond to look for frogs and maybe even duck eggs!

Grandma smiled at their happy faces. "Yes, but children, please be careful! I will pack a snack for you to take with you, and I will ring the lunch bell at noon. When you hear that bell, please come back right away. Do you understand?"

The children nodded their heads. Charlotte asked, "Grandma, what does your lunch bell sound like? I don't think I have ever seen it!" Grandma ducked into her pantry and came back out with a very strange looking contraption in her hand. It was metal and was shaped like this:

"This bell has been in my family since my grandfather settled this land many, many years ago. Do you know what this shape is, Charlotte?" Grandma said, holding the bell out for the children to inspect.

"Yes, Grandma! It's a triangle!" Charlotte answered.

"You are right! This is a triangle. It is called a triangle because the prefix 'tri' means 'three.' See, the bell has three sides, and three corners," Grandma explained to the children.

"But Grandma, how does it make noise?" Charlie asked. Grandma took a wooden rod off of the shelf where she had gotten the bell.

"You hold the bell by this rope that is attached at the top, and then you hit it with this wooden rod, like this," Grandma demonstrated for the children.

"Wow, that is really loud! I think we will be able to hear that even down at the pond!" Charlie exclaimed with his hands over his ears. Charlotte nodded in agreement.

Practice tracing these triangles.

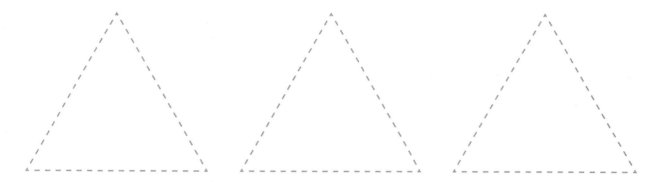

Now try drawing your own triangle!

A triangle can also look like this. As long as it has 3 sides and 3 corners, it is a triangle.

Color all of the rectangles blue. Color all of the circles green. Color all of the triangles yellow.

Write the numbers on the line below in order.

0   1   2   3   4

_____

- -

5   6   7   8   9

_____

- -

Charlie and Charlotte skipped through the tall grass down to the pond. They were so excited about their exploration! Grandma had given them a butterfly net and some old kitchen containers. They wanted to find frogs and butterflies, but mostly frogs!

The twins dropped down to rest at the edge of the pond. Nature was alive and chirping around them. It was so different here than at home, in town! They could hear Grandpa whistling as he worked on his tractor, and a strange sound reverberated through the trees.

"What a strange sound, Charlie! What do you think that is?" exclaimed Charlotte.

"I don't know! Maybe we could find out and catch whatever is making that noise!" Charlie jumped to his feet.

"Oh! Charlotte! Look! Look at what I found!" he said as he scooped up something in his hand and laid it carefully in his sister's lap.

"What is this? It looks like a giant, fuzzy worm! Look! Here's another one! And another!" Charlotte gasped with excitement. The funny little creatures were all over a large plant next to her. They looked like fat, green, black and yellow worms, and they had funny, little feelers sticking out of both ends! The children had never seen anything like them before.

The twins cautiously broke off a branch of the plant that had five of the funny creatures on it and very carefully placed the whole thing into their largest container. They decided to take it back to the house to show Grandma. She would know what they were!

Help the student count the other creatures and plants they found and write the number on the lines.

_____   _____   _____

_____   _____   _____

Using the shapes you have learned so far, draw a pattern! Color your pattern in a nice bright color. Explain the pattern to your teacher.

Numbers for copywork:

0   1   2   3   4

5   6   7   8   9

How many sides does a rectangle have? _____

   How many sides are short? _____

   How many sides are long? _____

How many corners does a rectangle have? _____

   Are they right angles? _____

Draw a rectangle here:

How many sides does a triangle have? _____

How many corners? _____

Draw a triangle here:

Does a circle have any corners? _____

Draw a circle here:

The children were having a wonderful time chasing butterflies and watching the ants trying to carry cookie crumbs that were much bigger than the ants themselves! The sound of Grandma's lunch bell startled them, and they quickly started to gather their nature treasures and snack bags.

Grandma had made chicken vegetable soup and peanut butter and jelly sandwiches from fresh, homemade bread. It was delicious. As the children ate, they told Grandma and Grandpa all about their discoveries at the pond.

"Grandpa, when we were down at the pond, we kept hearing a strange, chirpy sound, almost a buzzing, but really high and loud! What was that?" Charlotte asked between bites of her sandwich.

"That sound is made by the cicadas," Grandpa explained. "Cicadas are insects that have a very strange ability! The male cicadas have a part of their body, near their middle, that they can vibrate, which makes that sound." Grandpa picked up the lid to Grandma's homemade strawberry preserves. In the middle of the lid was a strange, little bubble that Grandpa pushed down. It made a small popping sound when he did this, and when he let it go, it popped again. "This is similar to what the cicadas do with that part of their body. When they do it really fast, it makes the sound you heard."

The twins' eyes were round with wonder. "That is so strange!" Charlotte exclaimed. "We also found some really, really funny things that look like giant worms. We left them on the porch in a container. May we show you?"

Grandma nodded with a smile, and the children darted to the porch and came back carrying the container between them. Grandpa and Grandma came over and knelt next to the box. The children carefully lifted one of the funny creatures out so they could all see it.

"Children, these are monarch caterpillars!" Grandpa exclaimed. "I haven't seen this many around the farm in a long, long time. This is very exciting!" The children looked at each other with puzzled expressions.

"What are caterpillars, Grandpa?" Charlotte asked. "We thought they were big, fuzzy worms."

Grandpa chuckled and pointed to a butterfly that the children had captured and brought home in another container. "That butterfly is a monarch. They are some of the most beautiful butterflies in the world! This 'fuzzy worm,' as you call it, is a 'baby' butterfly," Grandpa explained. The children were very surprised now!

"Baby butterflies? But they don't have any wings! How can they be butterflies?" They exclaimed together. They thought that maybe Grandpa was joking, because this seemed impossible.

Grandma came to the rescue when she said, "Come here, children, I will explain it all. Come sit down, and I will draw you a picture of how those little, fuzzy creatures with no wings will be baby butterflies." The children came to the table and watched as Grandma drew this picture.

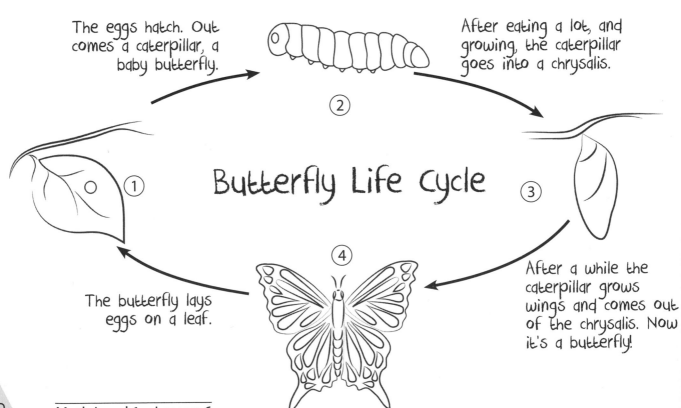

The eggs hatch. Out comes a caterpillar, a baby butterfly.

After eating a lot, and growing, the caterpillar goes into a chrysalis.

②

Butterfly Life Cycle

①

③

④

The butterfly lays eggs on a leaf.

After a while the caterpillar grows wings and comes out of the chrysalis. Now it's a butterfly!

"Can you see how God uses patterns all around us? There are many patterns in nature. We call these patterns 'life cycles.' They keep going and going! When a caterpillar goes into its chrysalis and then comes out as a butterfly, that butterfly will go and lay its eggs on a leaf. Those eggs will hatch, and out will come more caterpillars. So continues the pattern of a butterfly life cycle," Grandma explained.

"Grandpa, can you teach us more numbers?" Charlotte asked. "There were so many caterpillars, we didn't know how to count that many!"

Grandpa smiled. "Of course I will. I will show you tonight after supper. Right now I need to get back to work on that tractor." Grandpa scooped up his hat, and kissing each of the twins and Grandma goodbye, headed back to work.

Now it's your turn! Go exploring and see what patterns you can find!

Teacher

Patterns are all around you! Example: What comes after breakfast? Then what? Can you see the pattern that happens every day? Talk about this with your student. Number awareness and pattern awareness walk hand in hand.

Draw or tell your teacher some of the patterns you found!

Review Time! Help Charlie and Charlotte write a letter to their parents showing what they have learned.

Dear Mom and Dad,

We are having so much fun! We want to show you what we have learned.

Numbers for copywork:

0   1   2   3   4

5   6   7   8   9

There are patterns all around us! This is a pattern of shapes, including a new shape, the triangle. Draw what comes next.

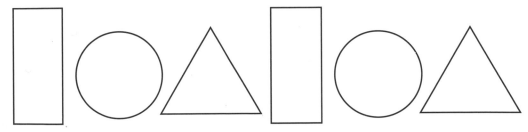

Learning to Count with Bigger Numbers – Place Values

We are going to be introducing the concept of place value in this lesson. Place value is a concept that takes time and patience to master. If your child does not understand it the first time they are introduced to it, please do not be concerned. We are going to be building their understanding slowly and in a hands-on, concrete fashion. I highly recommend reading the section in the Math Lesson For a Living Education Teaching Companion,* *about building numeric awareness through place value activities. In preparation for teaching this lesson (and other lessons about place value), you will need to gather these items:*

- At the back of this book, you will find several pages with your "Place Value Village." Cut out the "houses" and paste each piece on a separate piece of sturdy paper. You may want to laminate each "house" to make it more durable. You may also choose to use the Place Value Village Counting Mat too!

- Gather three cups or containers:

  > one smaller, shorter one (for the ONES' house)
  >
  > one medium one (for the TENS' house)
  >
  > one larger one (for the HUNDREDS' house)
  >
  > To create your Place Value Village set, adhere your houses onto the side of the containers.

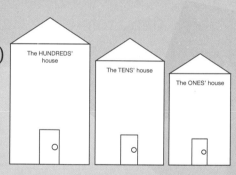

- Also have on hand numerous small items, such as dried beans (kidney beans work very well), ten snack-size baggies, and one one-gallon freezer bag.

Have your student use the Place Value Village to work through this lesson with the twins and their grandpa. As the story characters are dropping beans into the "houses," have your student do it also. Have them write the numbers and then place the beans in the baggie.

See Angela O'Dell's Place Value instructional video: www.youtube.com/watch?v=fuZ7Y3fDe7c

*The Math Lessons for a Living Education Teaching Companion is available in print or as a digital product at masterbooks.com.

The twins were excited. Grandpa had promised to tell them a story that would teach them about numbers larger than 9!

After supper, Grandpa invited the children to come sit with him in his big chair. "Children, you have learned a lot in the time you have been here! You have learned numbers all the way to 9, and you have learned about several shapes. I am very proud of how curious you both are," Grandpa said, giving each of them a squeeze. "Tonight, I am going to tell you a 'learning story.' This kind of story teaches you something, so it is very important to listen carefully. Do you have your listening ears on?"

Charlie and Charlotte giggled and showed Grandpa their ears. "Yes, Grandpa, they are on! See?" Grandpa pretended to inspect the children's ears, and nodded in satisfaction.

"Okay, I see your ears are on, so I will tell you the story. This is the same story I used to tell your daddy. In fact, he was about the same age you are right now when I told him! This story is very special because it teaches you how to count bigger numbers. If you can understand the pattern in numbers, you can continue counting on and on. Here, children, come sit over here by the coffee table. I want to be able to show you something important."

The children climbed down from Grandpa's lap and knelt beside the coffee table like Grandpa had asked. "Children, I want to show you what I call Place Value Village," Grandpa explained as he placed something rather odd looking on the table in front of the children. Charlie and Charlotte looked at each other with puzzled expressions. Grandpa smiled as he placed a large piece of paper in front of his "village" and handed each of the children a crayon. "You will understand soon, I promise!" There were three containers, and on the side of each was what looked like a little house! The one on the right was small, the one in the middle was medium sized, and the one on the left was large. Next, Grandpa placed one dried bean in the smallest container. "How many beans did I put in this container, children?"

"One!" the twins said together.

"That's right! One of you use your crayon and write the number 1 on this paper right here," Grandpa said pointing to the paper right in front of the ONES' house's door. Charlie carefully wrote a one on the paper as Grandpa instructed. "Now, children, as I continue placing beans in the ONES' house, you write the correct number right under the 1 that you wrote. Understand?"

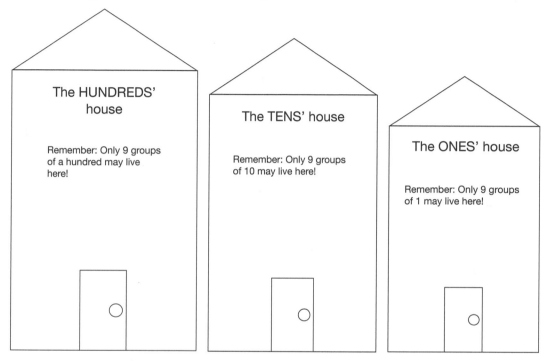

This is what the children wrote as Grandpa placed beans in the container:

0 1 2 3 4 5 6 7 8 9

"Mom taught us to count to the number 10...So 10 comes next!" Charlie declared.

"Yes, Charlie! In a way, we start over. You see, only 9 beans can live in this house. Only 9 groups of one bean. So after 9 comes the number 10. You know that 10 is written like this: 10. It has what we call two **digits** or two number spaces."

Grandpa emptied out the beans that he had placed in the ONES' house and placed another bean with them. "Now we have 10 beans! But not all of these beans can live in the ONES' house. They have to go live next door in the TENS'.

house. Like this." Grandpa had the children help him place the ten beans into a small baggy.

After they finished placing the ten beans in the baggy, Grandpa instructed them to place it into the TENS' house. "Now, children, let's practice writing the number 10. In the number 10, the 1 stands for 1 group of ten. See? And the 0 stands for nothing in the ONES' house. We have to have the 0 there to be a 'place holder.' " This is what Grandpa wrote on the paper:

HUNDREDS	TENS	ONES
		1
		2
		3
		4
		5
		6
		7
		8
		9
	1	0

"Do you understand, children?" Grandpa asked. The twins nodded. "We think we better practice this a while, Grandpa," Charlotte said. "We will understand it better if we do that."

Grandpa nodded his head and said, "It is very important to hear this story in stages. Because it is a learning story, we need to understand each part of the story before we move on to the next. Let's practice what I've shown you for now, and tomorrow I will tell you another part of the story."

You do the same!

Numbers for copywork:

0   1   2   3   4   5

6   7   8   9   10

Draw the correct number of circles next to the numbers. First one is done for you.

2

7

9

10

3

Practice using your Place Value Village to count beans.

Teacher

After your student is comfortable with counting to 10 and understands that the 1 stands for 1 group of 10, and the 0 stands for no ones, you may continue with the next part of the lesson. If your student needs more practice, please take the time to practice that concept until they can narrate back to you what they have learned, therefore showing you that they understand.

Teacher: "When we write the numbers 10, 11, 12, 13, 14, 15, 16, 17, 18, and 19, what does the 1 stand for?" Student: Allow student to tell you that it stands for 1 group of 10. Teacher: "And what do these numbers mean?" Student: Wait for them to tell you that they stand for groups of one, or that they are in the ONES' house. Give your student the number cards (0–19), and have your student put them in order from smallest to greatest. Have your student narrate back to you what they have learned about the tens' and ones' places.

Teacher

After you have practiced the concept of 10, move on to 11–19. Continue to add items to your ONES' house, and have your student write the numbers using washable markers, placing the one under the TENS' house on the laminated place value counting mat.

Like this:

TENS' house	ONES' house
	1
	2
	3
	4
	5
	6
	7
	8
	9
1	0
1	1
1	2
1	3
1	4
1	5
1	6
1	7
1	8
1	9

Numbers for copywork:

0 1 2 3 4

5 6 7 8 9

10 11 12 13 14

15 16 17 18 19

10 11 12 13 14

15 16 17 18 19

Help the little triangle to get through the maze.
Only the doors with the triangle shape can be opened.

More Work with Place Values

The next morning, Grandpa asked, "Would you children like to help harvest some carrots? Every Thursday afternoon, I set up a stand to sell vegetables at the farmers' market in town. I've had several requests for my sweet baby carrots."

The children both nodded their heads, "We would love to, Grandpa, but you will have to show us how." They remembered that carrots are a root vegetable, which means the part to eat is under the ground. They had seen Grandpa use a pitchfork to dig some up for Grandma's veggie soup.

"I will show you how to dig them up and how to bundle them," Grandpa told the children. "Make sure you have garden gloves on. This is a dirty job!" The children raced to the porch and found their gloves. "Oh, and Children, ask Grandma for a bag of rubber bands, please!" called Grandpa from the door. "We will need them to bundle the carrots."

The children took the bag of bands from Grandma and went to Grandpa, who was gathering the needed tools from the tool shed. The children watched in awe as Grandpa carefully placed the pitchfork alongside the green, leafy tops of the carrots. With one smooth movement, he pushed back on the handle of the fork, and out came the carrots!

"Charlie, you and Charlotte gather these up and shake the loose dirt off, please," Grandpa instructed the children. "We want to bundle them in groups of ten, like this." He showed them how to gather the carrots by their green tops, and then wrap a rubber band around them — close to where the stem connected to the carrot. "Be careful not to snap yourselves with the band, and try not to break the green top," Grandpa smiled at the looks of concentration on the children's faces. "Children, remember what I taught you last night about counting? We practiced counting up to 19 items. Look, when we have one bundle of 10, and we have 9 more carrots; that is 19, right?" The children nodded their heads. "If we put one more carrot with the other 9, we have another group of 10, see?" Again, the children nodded. "When we have 2 groups of 10, that makes 20." The children looked a little puzzled at this information. "If we were using our Place Value Village, we would have 2 groups of 10 in the TENS' house, and 0 items in the ONES' house. Like this:

HUNDREDS' house	TENS' house	ONES' house
		1
		2
		3
		4
		5
		6
		7
		8
		9
	1	0
	1	1
	1	2
	1	3
	1	4
	1	5
	1	6
	1	7
	1	8
	1	9
	2	0

Two groups of 10 is 20. The 2 in the TENS' house stands for 2 groups of 10. And the 0 is a place holder in the ONES' house."

The children want to practice counting up to 20. They need practice working with their Place Value Village. It takes practice to understand some concepts well. Let's practice!

Teacher

Have your student use the Place Value Village and mat to practice counting items up to 20. Have them narrate to you what they are doing.

Numbers for copywork:

10 11 12 13 14 15

Put all the numbers 0–20 in order using the number cards from our last lesson. Talk about any patterns you see in the numbers.

Have your students use the Place Value Village and mat to practice counting items up to 20. Have them narrate to you what they are doing. Try not to coach them in counting and writing — let them show you what they know!

Numbers for copywork:

16 17 18 19 20

_____

- -

_____

Put all the numbers 0–20 in order using the number cards from our last lesson. Talk about any patterns you see in the numbers.

Teacher

Have your student use the Place Value Village and mat to practice counting items up to 20. Have them narrate to you what they are doing. Try to use various objects to count.

Numbers for copywork:

0 1 2 3 4 5

6 7 8 9 10

Using the shapes you have learned so far, make a pattern in the space below. Talk about your pattern. Did you use a pattern of colors also?

 My pattern:

What comes before? (If you need to, use your 100's Chart in the back of the book.)

_____, 10   _____, 5

_____, 7   _____, 2

_____, 19   _____, 18

_____, 4   _____, 15

_____, 1   _____, 11

Review Time!

Teacher

This is the big day. Make it feel like a big and important event. Ask your student to help decorate for their big show and tell. Make a poster or a sign announcing the show time, and bake/buy a special dessert to celebrate your student's success. Let your student know what a big deal this is to you by taking time to celebrate!

There are spaces on the next page to paste pictures of your student giving their big show and tell. On the lines below, make a few notes about it. How did they do? Did they clearly show their understanding? Are there any areas that need work?

_____

_____

_____

_____

_____

_____

_____

Math Level 1 – Lesson 8

This week we are going to help the twins write letters to their parents. They are so excited about everything they have been learning! There are five sections; one for each day. Please help students write out what they have learned.

Dear Mom and Dad,

Charlotte and I want to show you what we have been learning!

Love, Charlotte, Charlie, and our friend _____

Numbers for copywork:

0 1 2 3 4 5

6 7 8 9 10

Draw the correct number of circles next to the numbers. The first one is done for you.

3 ◯ ◯ ◯

5

10

7

4

Numbers for copywork:

10 11 12 13 14 15

16 17 18 19 20

Write what comes before:

_____ , 5

_____ , 8

_____ , 11

_____ , 20

_____ , 3

Write what comes after:

12, _____

9, _____

17, _____

14, _____

Draw a rectangle:

Draw a triangle:

Draw a circle:

Draw a picture of your Place Value Village.

 My Place Value Village:

How many groups of 1 may live in the ONE'S house? _____

How many groups of 10 may live in the TEN'S house? _____

Use your number cards to put the numbers 0–20 in order.

Use your Place Value Village to count 20 items. Write the numbers here as you count them.

HUNDREDS' house	TENS' house	ONES' house

In the numbers 10, 11, 12, 13, 14, 15, 16, 17, 18, and 19, the 1 stands for a group of

_____.

Review Time! Using all of the shapes you have learned so far, draw a pattern and color it with bright colors.

 My pattern:

Numbers for copywork:

10 11 12 13 14 15

16 17 18 19 20

? ? ? ?

HOW MANY?

Place Value, Patterns of 10s

"Can you believe how much we have learned so far?" the twins asked their grandparents while they sat around the kitchen table eating supper. "We have learned so much about numbers, and gardens, and animals, and, and well . . . and everything!"

Grandma smiled at them. "You really have learned a lot, children. And guess what? You are going to learn even more! How would you like to help me with something really special tomorrow morning?" Grandma asked.

"Do you need more help with your egg orders, Grandma?" asked Charlie before he stuck a large mouthful of apple pie into his mouth.

Grandma refilled his milk glass before answering. "Charlie, please don't put so much in your mouth at one time. You could choke! And no, I don't need help with egg orders. This time, I need help with my flowers. I have a friend whose granddaughter is getting married on Saturday, the day after tomorrow. My friend has asked me to supply the flowers for the wedding. I am very excited and happy about this! My tulips and hyacinths are the most beautiful ones I've ever grown, and I need your help cutting them. Do you think you and Charlotte could help me? We have to be very, very careful. Flowers are fragile."

The children nodded with big eyes. "Yes, Grandma, we want to help."

"Okay, after breakfast tomorrow morning, you two be ready to help. We have to cut them, and then I am going to arrange them in groups of 10. There are going to be 8 flower arrangements, one for each bridesmaid, and 2 corsages for the mothers. I also have grown 6 large pots of flowers that Grandpa is going to put into the back of the pickup truck and take to the church tomorrow."

The next morning, the children were ready to help Grandma with the flowers. She handed them each a pair of scissors, and after stopping at the tool shed for buckets, they all walked out to the flower gardens. Grandma had gorgeous

flowers. The tulips were all different shades of pink, yellow, red, and even purple! They were Charlie's favorite. Charlotte especially liked the hyacinths with their tall blossom-decked stems. They smelled sweet too! They watched as fat bumblebees, laden down with almost more pollen than they could carry, flew from blossom to blossom.

Grandma explained how to carefully cut the flowers and place them, stem-side down, into the buckets of water. After a while, they had five buckets full of flowers, and Grandma told them that it was enough. She asked the children to help line up the buckets so Grandpa could bring them to the house for them.

Back in the kitchen, Grandma washed her hands, then took three plates out of the cupboard and placed two soft, homemade, oatmeal raisin cookies on each. She placed one in front of each of the children and poured them each a glass of cold milk.

"Children, did you know that tulips and hyacinths grow back every year? I do not have to plant them each spring. They are what we call perennials. They grow from 'bulbs' like this. Each fall I cut their stems close to the ground and cover them with straw to keep them from getting too cold."

After they were finished with their snacks, the twins helped Grandma line up flower vases filled with water. Grandpa brought the buckets of flowers in, and Grandma showed the children how to make bundles with 10 flowers in each. They had already learned from Grandpa that 2 groups of 10 is 20. Look at your 100's Chart. Point to these numbers as your teacher reads them out loud: 0, 10, 20, 30, 40, 50, 60, 70, 80, 90. Talk about the pattern you see. What do all of these numbers end in?

Now they counted:

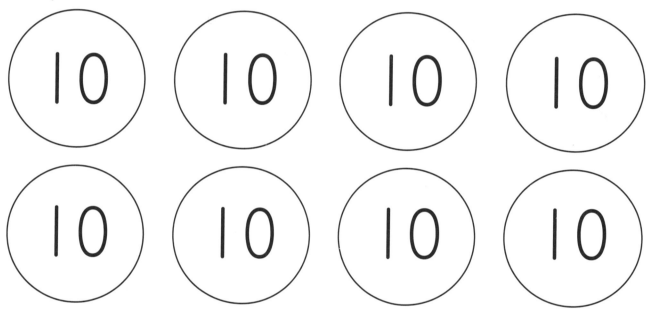

How many groups of 10 are there?

So 8 groups of 10 is "80." That means 8 groups of 10 and 0 groups of 1. In our Place Value Village it would look like this:

HUNDREDS' house	TENS' house	ONES' house
	8	0

Practice counting groups of 10. Remember, if there are no ones, we put a 0 in the ONE'S house.

Teacher

Practice counting by 10s with your students.

Practice counting groups of 10.

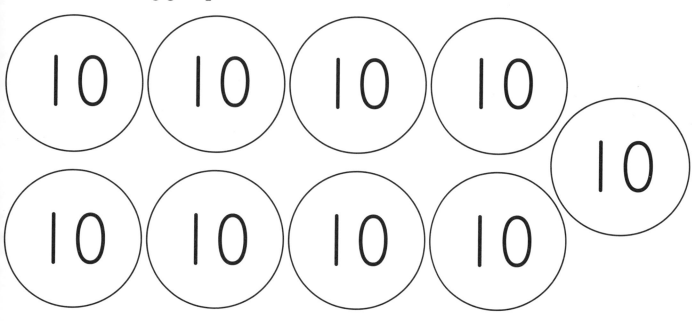

How many groups of 10? _____   How many groups of 1? _____

Numbers for copywork:

20 21 22 23 24

25 26 27 28 29

Teacher

Help your student count 30 items using their Place Value Village. Have them write the numbers on their Place Value Village Counting Mat. At the end of Exercise 3, do not erase the numbers written today; we will be adding to them throughout the week. Make sure to remind your student that the digit in the tens' place stands for groups of 10. Try to find everyday things around you that show these higher numbers and point them out to your student. It is by building the habit of awareness that we instill critical thinking in our children.

Numbers for copywork:

30 31 32 33 34

35 36 37 38 39

Using your 100's chart, point to the 10s as your teacher reads them out loud.

Name_____

Numbers for copywork:

40 41 42 43 44

45 46 47 48 49

In the space below, use the shapes you have learned to make a picture. Color it and show it to your class or family.

 My picture:

Teacher

Help your student count 10 more items using the Place Value Village, bringing it up to 50 items counted. Have them write the numbers on their Place Value Village Counting Mat. At the end of Exercise 5, do not erase the numbers written today; your student is going to use them to narrate to you at the end of this exercise.

Numbers for copywork:

50 51 52 53 54

55 56 57 58 59

Review Time!

Teacher

Invite your student to show what they have learned this week. Encourage them to show the numbers they have written on their Place Value Village Counting Mat. If you need to help them, that's okay. Confidence is built when they feel your encouragement. Talk about the 1, 2, 3, 4, 5 pattern that is in every group of 10. Example: 21, 22, 23, 24, 25, or 41, 42, 43, 44, 45. If your student can understand this pattern, it will make it much easier for them.

Show and tell notes:

_____

_____

Practice with Patterns and Shapes

"Grandpa, can you tell us more about patterns in nature?" Charlotte asked that evening. The twins had helped Grandma arrange bouquets of flowers, and the kitchen counters were covered in the beautiful, sweet-smelling blossoms. The twins were dressed for bed and rather sleepy! Grandpa had brought out his old, homemade tic-tac-toe game board, and the twins were kneeling in front of the fireplace playing game after game.

"Well, what kind of patterns would you like to learn about, Charlotte?" Grandpa responded, looking over the rim of his reading glasses. Charlie liked it when he did that; it reminded him of Daddy. "The kind that Grandma said is all around us," Charlie piped up. "You know, like Grandma drew us a picture of how a caterpillar becomes a butterfly."

Grandpa nodded his head, "Oh, that kind of pattern! Okay, children, bring me that sketchpad over there, and the box of crayons and pencils. I will draw you some pictures."

This is the first pattern Grandpa drew:

What comes after:

4, _____

9, _____

14, _____

17, _____

6, _____

What comes before:

_____, 18

_____, 11

_____, 16

_____, 8

_____, 1

Numbers for copywork:

20 21 22 23 24

25 26 27 28 29

Then he drew this.
Finish the picture by coloring it.

 ———→  ———→

Put the numbers 0–20 in order using your number cards.

Use your Place Value Village, and count 39 items. Write the numbers on your Place Value Village Counting Mat. Explain the numbers to your teacher. How many items did you count?

Tens _____   Ones _____   How many? _____

Numbers for copywork:

30 31 32 33 34

35 36 37 38 39

After you are finished copying the numbers above, point to each one and say it out loud.

Next, he drew this:

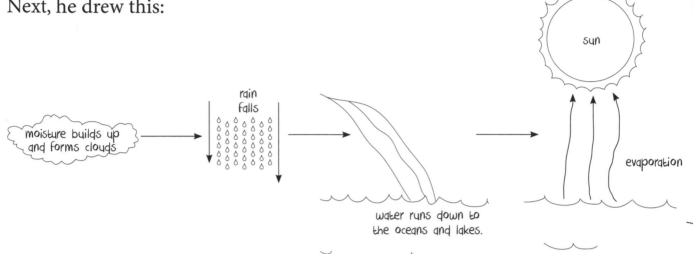

Count the groups of 10.

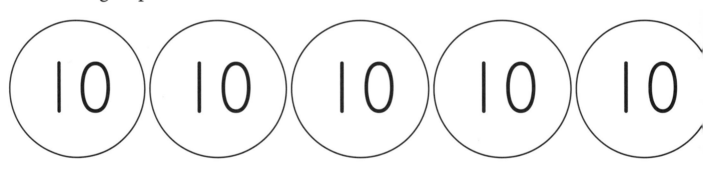

How many 10s?_____ How many 1s? _____ write the number _____

Numbers for copywork:

10 20 30 40 50

Make a picture using all the shapes you have learned so far. Send the picture to someone you love. Have your teacher help you write a letter, and in your letter, show what you have learned about numbers. Make sure you show them how to count groups of 10!

 My picture:

Write the name of the person to whom you sent your card.

_____

Review Time!

Show and tell and celebrate learning!

Have the student orally narrate everything they have learned this week. Let them use their pictures of the patterns in nature as they show what they have learned.

Supply them with multiple small items, their Place Value Village, and their 100's chart. Have the student show others in the class or their family what they have learned about counting items using the terms "10s" and "1s."

Have the student show others in the class or their family the pattern of 10s on the 100's chart.

Color this for fun!

Introducing the + and = Symbols

Teacher

Over the course of this week, have the student orally narrate everything they have learned this week. Let them use their pictures of the patterns in nature as they show what they have learned.

Supply them with multiple small items, their Place Value Village, and their 100's chart. Have the student show others in the class or their family what they have learned about counting items using the terms "10s" and "1s."

Have the student show others in the class or their family the pattern of 10s on the 100's chart.

One lazy morning, the children were playing on the rope swing, which hung from the barn rafters. As Charlie gave his sister a push, Grandpa called from the stall at the other end of the barn, "Children, quick! Come and see! Betsy has had her babies!" With a squeal, the twins abandoned the swing and ran to where Grandpa was kneeling in the straw.

"Grandpa! Can we see? Can we see?" the twins chimed together. Betsy was the mama sheep whom the twins had been caring for since their arrival. She had gotten bigger and bigger as the lambs inside of her had grown. Grandpa had told them that Betsy had had two babies the year before also . . . twins! He had promised Charlie and Charlotte that they could have these two babies.

As the twins bent down, they saw the most darling lambs! They were so tiny! "When were they born, Grandpa?" Charlotte asked as she stroked the babies' heads. Grandpa sat back on his heels as he patted Betsy on the head.

"They must have been born last night, Charlotte. It must have been during that storm we had, because I would have heard otherwise. You two take these babies and sit over there. I need to make sure everything is okay with Betsy."

The twins carefully picked up the babies and moved a few feet away, so Grandpa could check Betsy over. "She looks fine! Thank goodness! I like to be with the sheep when they have their young ones. She just looks tired. Bring her babies back over now, so they can nurse and sleep." Grandpa took the babies from the children and carefully placed them back by Betsy. "This one is a girl . . . and let's see what this one is . . . a boy! We have a boy and a girl just like you two!" Grandpa smiled at the children's happy expressions. "Betsy is a good mama! These two babies plus the other babies she had last year. . . ." Grandpa counted on his fingers, "that makes four babies in all. Children, let's go tell Grandma about this. A little later, I will show you how I figured out how many babies Betsy has had."

Grandma was happy to hear about Betsy's babies. She smiled at the children's excitement as she placed the plates on the table for lunch. "You know, children, Betsy had two babies last year too!" The children nodded. "Why don't you two go wash your hands and get ready for lunch now," Grandma told the children.

As they sat down to their lunch, the children were practically bouncing in excitement. It's not every day that you get to hold a lamb!

Grandpa smiled as they chattered about the babies in the barn, "Children, I want to show you how to add. That means putting more than one set of items together and then counting all of the items together."

ame_____

 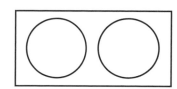

Like this:

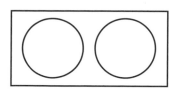

There are two circles in each set. If we count them together, we have 4 circles all together. We use these symbols when we are writing this on paper:

+ and =

So we would write 2 and 2 is 4 like this:

2 + 2 = 4

Trace the symbols below:

+ means "and." When you see this symbol, you know you are going to be adding sets of items together.

= means "the same as" or "equal." When you see this symbol, you know that the number or sets on both sides are exactly the same.

Trace these addition "problems."

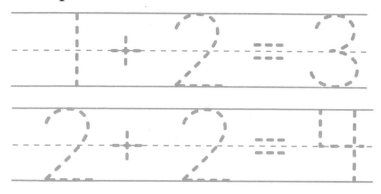

Practice adding these sets. Write the number of items in each set, then write the answer.

_____ + _____ = _____

_____ + _____ = _____

_____ + _____ = _____

Numbers for copywork:

30 31 32 33 34

35 36 37 38 39

Draw pictures to solve these addition problems.

Example

3 ◯ + 2 ◯ = ___5___

2 ◯ + 5 ◯ = _____

2 ◯ + 1 ◯ = _____

4 ◯ + 2 ◯ = _____

ame________________________________

Exercise 3 Day 58

Teacher

Have your student use the Place Value Village and Place Value Village Counting Mat to practice counting items up to 50. Have them narrate to you what they are doing.

Numbers for copywork:

40 41 42 43 44

45 46 47 48 49

Take out the "My Addition Mat" in the manipulative section of this book and the 0–20 number cards. From the 0–8 cards, choose 2 number cards at a time to make your own addition problems. Use beans, buttons, or some other small objects to solve your problems. As you work, tell your teacher what you are doing and why. Study the example.

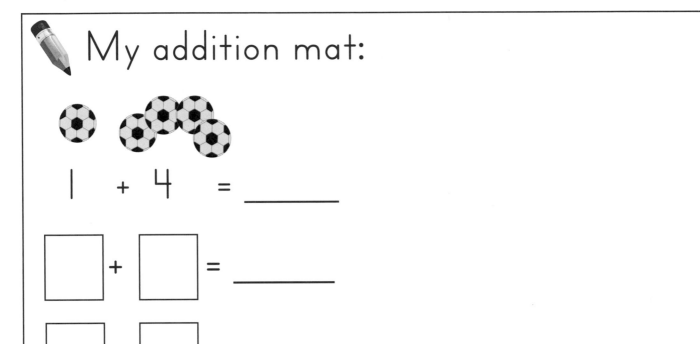

✏️ My addition mat:

1 + 4 = _____

☐ + ☐ = _____

☐ + ☐ = _____

Using all the shapes you have learned, draw and color a pattern.

✏️ My pattern:

Review Time!

Help the twins show their parents what they have learned.

Dear Mom and Dad,

Guess what? Betsy had her lambs! Grandpa gave them to us as pets. May we please bring them home with us? Please! Please! Grandpa also taught us about addition. Look what we can do. (Use your Addition Mat)

$2 + 3 =$ _____ $5 + 2 =$ _____

$4 + 2 =$ _____ $1 + 7 =$ _____

We can also write these numbers now. (Write the number you say when you count the 10s. You may look at your 100's chart if you need to.)

_____

- - - - - - - - - - - - - - - - - -

_____

- - - - - - - - - - - - - - - - - -

_____

Last week, Grandpa taught us more about patterns in nature! This is our favorite! (Choose your favorite and draw it for the twins' parents.)

 My pattern:

Love,

Charlie, Charlotte, and our friend, _____

Addition + 1

The twins were having so much fun playing with their new little lambs. The babies seemed to be growing over night! Charlotte had named her little female (girl) lamb, Ann. Charlie decided Andy was a good name for his male (boy) lamb. As the lambs got a little bigger, the children were allowed to bring them outside to play in the yard. Grandma chuckled as she watched the children rolling around on the ground. The lambs loved the game and pranced and jumped about, kicking their heels up in the air. The children giggled when the lambs nibbled on their hair.

"I declare, those lambs are getting fuzzier every day!" Grandma murmured to herself one day, as she watched them from the kitchen window. "They are starting to look like little fluff-balls! And the children love them so much!" She was happy to see her grandchildren growing so tan and strong. Their clothes were a little more stained than when they had first come to the farm, and their faces were freckled and sun-kissed. Grandma sighed, "They're growing as fast as the lambs! And this visit is going faster than I ever thought it would. Oh, hello, Pokey! Did you finally decide to wake up and join the rest of the world?"

Pokey stopped and looked up at Grandma. He spent most of the time in his box by the kitchen stove, or right outside the back door in an old baby playpen. The children had decided to make a place for him there. They were a little worried about him wandering off to the pond in the back pasture. He certainly didn't mind! He liked to sit and sun himself on the rocks that the children had placed in the old pen for him. And when he was in the kitchen, Grandma was always giving him bits and pieces of lettuce, carrots, or even green onion tops! Pokey had never tasted anything so delicious in his life! Yes, Pokey had decided that country life was the life for him.

Grandma smiled at Pokey as he wandered out to the back porch and worked his way through the cat-door in the bottom of the back door. He had discovered he could let himself in and out that way. His playpen was positioned at the edge of the porch, and he could easily

climb up and down the rocks to get in and out. He seemed to like this arrangement.

After taking the last tray of molasses cookies out of the oven, Grandma poured two glasses of ice-cold milk and placed them on the table. Going to the door, she called to the children to return Ann and Andy to their mother in the barn, then come in and wash up for snack time.

The children ran to obey, and when they came in, Charlotte exclaimed, "Oh, Grandma, molasses cookies? I love those! How many may we have?" Grandma smiled but said, "Zero, until you wash your hands! Then you may have two." The children giggled and ran to obey, coming back to the table with clean hands.

Charlie tried not to gobble his cookie. Grandma was always admonishing him to slow down and take smaller bites. He still finished faster than his sister and Grandma. "May I have another one, Grandma?" he asked, trying to be as polite as possible.

Grandma chuckled, "Charlie, you have a big appetite, don't you! Yes, you may have one more. You have had 2 already, so if you eat another one it will be 2 + 1 which equals 3." She handed both children one more cookie. "Children, knowing how to + 1 is an important skill. I will show you." Grandma placed one cookie on a plate. "This is 1 cookie. If I add another cookie, it will be 2 cookies. What if I add another cookie? How many cookies will it be?"

"It will be 3 cookies, Grandma," Charlotte answered "and if you put another cookie on the plate it will be 4 cookies! But who is going to eat all those cookies?"

"I will!" Charlie volunteered, "I could eat all of them." Grandma chuckled.

Study the pattern below and write the number on the line. The first one is done for you. This is the + 1 pattern. We use this pattern when we count by ones.

|

Use your Addition Mat to solve these addition equations.* Write the answers in the boxes. Then write out your own equations below in the space provided.

*Equation: a number "sentence" that uses an equal sign (=) to show 2 equal items. Example: ☺ + ☺ = 2 smiley faces

Do you see that both sides of our "equation" are equal?

$3 + 3 =$ ☐ $2 + 4 =$ ☐

$5 + 1 =$ ☐ $5 + 3 =$ ☐

$7 + 2 =$ ☐ $4 + 3 =$ ☐

You might also use beans on your Place Value Village Counting Mat to see the answer yourself.

Teacher

Help your student count 30 items using the Place Value Village. Have them write the numbers on their Place Value Village mat. Discuss the + 1 pattern that you are using. Do not erase the numbers your student writes on their mat. We will be adding more numbers later this week.

Numbers for copywork (say the numbers as you write them):

20 21 22 23 24

25 26 27 28 29

Use your addition mat to solve these addition equations. Narrate* to your teacher what you are doing and why. Write your answers in the box.

*Narrating or telling your teacher what you are doing helps you understand better. It is very important to understand the WHY in mathematics.

$4 + 3 = \boxed{}$ $2 + 5 = \boxed{}$

$8 + 1 = \boxed{}$ $5 + 3 = \boxed{}$

$6 + 2 = \boxed{}$ $4 + 4 = \boxed{}$

Name____________________________

Exercise 3

Day 63

Draw circles by each number showing how many?

1 ____________________________

2 ____________________________

3 ____________________________

4 ____________________________

5 ____________________________

6 ____________________________

7 ____________________________

8 ____________________________

9 ____________________________

10 ____________________________

Count and write how many are in each group.

      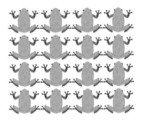

_____   _____   _____

Numbers for copywork (say the numbers as you write them):

30 31 32 33 34

35 36 37 38 39

Review Time!

Write the addition sign. _____

Write the equal sign. _____

What do we do when we add? (Narrate to your teacher)

What does the equal sign mean? (Narrate to your teacher)

Explain what the + 1 pattern is. (Narrate to your teacher)

Choose number cards with numbers 0–10 and, using your Addition Mat and small counting items, show your teacher what you know about addition.

Numbers for copywork (say the numbers as you write them):

40 41 42 43 44

45 46 47 48 49

Solve the equations so you can color the butterfly!

$2 + 1 =$ 3

$1 + 0 =$ 0

$1 + 1 =$ 2

$1 + 4 =$ 5

$1 + 3 =$ 4

$3 + 3 =$ 6

One day, as the children were helping Grandma hang sheets and towels on the clothesline, Charlotte asked, "Grandma, do you wash the sheets and towels every week?"

Grandma smiled around the clothes-pin in her mouth and nodded. After she had placed the clothes-pin on the edge of the sheet, she answered Charlotte, "Yes, I do, Honey. In fact, I usually do it on the same day of the week. That is, unless it is raining. In the spring and summer, I wait until I have a sunny day. I don't like using the clothes dryer in the summer, and I like the smell of the fresh air on the sheets."

"Grandma, could you remind us about the days of the week?" Charlie asked as he stood on tiptoe to reach the clothesline. Grandma smiled at his attempt to hang a towel. It hung crookedly from the line, with one edge almost touching the ground. But she did not redo it; she knew that Charlie had done his best, and that was good enough for her!

"I will, Charlie. Do you remember our song that helps us learn them? 'Row, row, row your boat'?" The children nodded. "Let's sing it again with each of the days of the week: 'Sunday, Monday, Tuesday, Wednesday, Thursday, Friday, Saturday! These are the seven days that make up a week!' Sing it with me!"

With a little practice, the children were singing along with Grandma. "That really does make it easier to remember, Grandma!" Charlie exclaimed. "Now we will always remember them!" You can learn the days of the week also!

Using the "Days of the Week" cards from the manipulative section of this book, practice placing the days in order. Sing the song Grandma sang with the twins. Trace the names of the days of the week.

How many days in a week are there? _____

What day is today? _____

What day(s) do you go to church? _____

Look at a calendar and look up what day your birthday falls on this year.

_____

Addition Practice

Use your Addition Mat (horizontal) and counting items to solve these equations. Narrate to your teacher what you are doing, and why you are doing it.

$5 + 3 =$ _____ $2 + 6 =$ _____

$9 + 1 =$ _____ $5 + 3 =$ _____

$7 + 3 =$ _____ $4 + 5 =$ _____

Do these exercises using your 100's Chart.

1. Place a small counting item on all the 10s; explain the pattern.

2. Find the number 15. What comes before? What comes after?

3. Find the number 8. What is 2 more? (Instruct your student to move his finger ahead 2 numbers.)

4. Find the number 4. What is 3 more?

5. Find the number 5. What is 1 more?

6. Find the number 45. What comes before? What comes after?

7. Find the number 50. What comes before? What comes after?

8. Repeat with these numbers: 20, 42, 55, and 80.

9. Find the number 11. What does each digit stand for?

10. Have your student narrate everything he or she can remember about the tens' place and the ones' place.

Numbers for copywork (say the numbers as you write them):

50 51 52 53 54

55 56 57 58 59

Using your "Days of the Week" cards, practice placing the days in order. Sing the song Grandma taught the twins.

Use your Addition Mat (horizontal) and counting items to solve these equations. Narrate to your teacher what you are doing and why you are doing it.

$7 + 3 =$ _____ $2 + 8 =$ _____

$2 + 1 =$ _____ $6 + 3 =$ _____

$3 + 3 =$ _____ $4 + 4 =$ _____

Numbers for copywork:

O   1   2   3   4

5   6   7   8   9

Using your "Days of the Week" cards, practice placing the days in order. Sing the song Grandma taught the twins.

Practice counting the groups of 10.

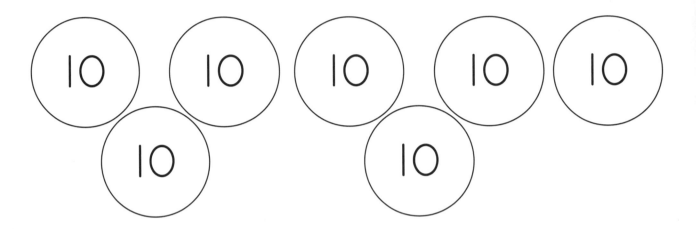

How many 10s?_____ How many 1s? _____ write the number _____

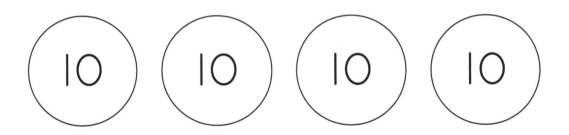

How many 10s?_____ How many 1s? _____ write the number _____

Ask your teacher for a clean sheet of white paper, and three different colors of construction paper. Draw and cut out rectangles, circles, and triangles in different colors. Make a pattern by pasting them onto the white paper.

Review Time! Help the twins write a letter to their parents.

Dear Mom and Dad,

Grandma taught us the days of the week! It's a lot of fun to sing the song she taught us about them. We will sing it to you the next time you call us. Last week, she taught us a new pattern. When we count with ones, we use the + 1 pattern. It goes like this:

You can see that each line of smiley faces has one more in it.

We can write all the numbers from 0–20. (Help the twins write the numbers. Try not to look back.)

How many are in each set?

😊 😊 😊 😊 😊 😊
😊 😊 😊 😊 😊 😊

_____   _____

Love, Charlie, Charlotte, and our friend _____

More About Addition (Vertical Addition)

"Did you two know that you can use dominoes to learn about numbers?" Grandpa asked the children. All three of them were on their hands and knees setting up a long, snaking line of dominoes. The line started in the kitchen and went around the corner and down the hall. The children couldn't wait to tip them all over! They had done this before with Grandpa. In fact, it had turned out to be their favorite Sunday afternoon game. Today was a good day to play dominoes, for it was storming outside and cozy inside. A fire crackled in the fireplace. It wasn't a big fire; just the right size to take the dampness out of the air, Grandma had said.

"How do you use them to learn about numbers, Grandpa?" Charlie asked. He was always amazed when Grandpa pointed out pattern, shapes, and numbers all around them.

"Do you see these little dots?" Grandpa asked. The children nodded. They had indeed seen the dots. "If you look at a domino, it's almost like looking at an addition problem. See? These dots up here are the top set, and these dots here are the bottom set."

You can line numbers up this way to add. Like this:

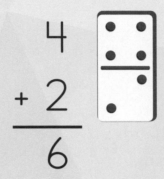

$$\begin{array}{r} 4 \\ +\ 2 \\ \hline 6 \end{array}$$

"You see, children, you are adding a group of 4 ones, and a group of 2 ones, and coming up with a group of 6 ones. You are learning that there are numbers, shapes, and patterns all around us. It is wise to always be observant to our surroundings. Come, let's look at some of these other dominoes. Each one of them is like an addition problem."

The children studied the dominoes in Grandpa's hand. "Grandpa, you are so smart," Charlotte said in wonder. "How did you get so smart?"

Grandpa chuckled and tousled her hair. "Oh, I'm not all that smart, Charlotte, I just like to learn. When I want to know more about something, I will research until I find the answer. Come on, let's finish setting these dominoes up. I can't wait to see them all go over!"

Teacher

We are going to start memorizing some math facts. Take the time now to look over making "right-brain" flashcards in the appendix. This is an important step for students. Some may become frustrated with memorization, so make it a game, and include them in on the activity of making their flashcards. Spend today's lesson having fun together with this activity. On one side of the flashcard, write the equation horizontally and on the other, vertically. The My Addition Mat (vertical) in the manipulatives section can help students with this concept. Use this as often as you wish. There is a section of extremely helpful tips about the making of right-brain flashcards and memorizing math facts in the Math Teaching Companion.

These are the facts for the flashcards.

Vertically:

$$\begin{array}{r} 2 \\ + 2 \\ \hline 4 \end{array} \qquad \begin{array}{r} 3 \\ + 3 \\ \hline 6 \end{array} \qquad \begin{array}{r} 3 \\ + 1 \\ \hline 4 \end{array} \qquad \begin{array}{r} 4 \\ + 1 \\ \hline 5 \end{array}$$

Horizontally:

$2 + 2 = 4 \qquad\qquad 3 + 1 = 4$

$3 + 3 = 6 \qquad\qquad 4 + 1 = 5$

Using your flashcards, have fun drilling your facts.

Numbers for copywork (say the numbers as you write them):

20 21 22 23 24

20 21 22 23 24

25 26 27 28 29

25 26 27 28 29

What comes before?

___8___, 9   ___11___, 12   ___19___, 20

___6___, 7   ___17___, 16

What comes after?

17, ___18___   23, ___22___   34, ___33___

57, ___47___   10, ___9___

Use your flashcards to review and drill your facts.

Practice adding. Use your small counting objects to solve the equations.

$$\begin{array}{r} 2 \\ +\ 1 \\ \hline 3 \end{array} \qquad \begin{array}{r} 3 \\ +\ 1 \\ \hline 4 \end{array} \qquad \begin{array}{r} 4 \\ +\ 1 \\ \hline 5 \end{array} \qquad \begin{array}{r} 5 \\ +\ 1 \\ \hline 6 \end{array} \qquad \begin{array}{r} 6 \\ +\ 1 \\ \hline 7 \end{array}$$

Use the space below to draw a pattern using the shapes you have learned so far. Explain your pattern to your teacher.

 My Pattern

Use your flashcards to review your math facts.

Using your Place Value Village and Place Value Village Counting Mat, count 45 objects. Narrate to your teacher what you are doing.

How many groups of 10 do you have? _____

How many groups of one? _____

Write the number here _____

Now count 27 objects. Narrate to your teacher what you are doing.

How many groups of 10 do you have? _____

How many groups of one?_____

Write the number here _____

Numbers for copywork (say the numbers as you write them):

40 41 42 43 44 45

Show your teacher these numbers on your 100's Chart.

Trace the days of the week.

Sunday

Monday

Tuesday

Wednesday

Thursday

Friday

Saturday

Numbers for copywork (say the numbers as you write them):

50 51 52 53 54

55 56 57 58 59

Show your teacher these numbers on your 100's Chart.

 Review Time! Write some addition facts that you learned this week.

More Addition; Introducing Squares

"Charlie, could you please come help me in the barn?" Grandpa asked as Grandma and Charlotte cleared the table after lunch one day. "I need a hand with a few projects, and I think you are big and strong enough to be a great help."

Charlie stood a little straighter and taller. "Yes, of course I can help you, Grandpa," he said in a very grown-up voice, "I am getting rather big, you know!" Grandpa's eyes twinkled as he smiled down at his little grandson.

"That you are, Charlie! That you are. I think you've grown a foot since you've been here!" Grandpa teased him. "I'm going to have to stack bricks on your head to keep you from growing so fast. What are you staring at, Charlie?" Grandpa looked puzzled, as Charlie was staring down at his feet.

"I haven't grown another foot, Grandpa! I've always had the same two feet!" Charlie said in a confused voice. Grandpa laughed so hard that he slapped his knee.

"Oh Charlie! That's not what I meant! I meant that you have grown a lot in the time you have been here!" Grandpa chuckled and chortled to himself as he laced up his work boots. "Grown another foot! Hee hee hee!" Charlie still looked a little confused, but since Grandpa was laughing, he decided he would laugh along with him.

"Grandpa, what do you need help with in the barn?" Charlie asked, deciding to change the subject. "Are you building something?" Grandpa was always building or moving something about in the barn.

"Yes, I need to either repair or replace the feeding troughs in two of the horse stalls. I noticed yesterday that they were needing some work," Grandpa answered. "I have some wooden crates

that I think I can use until I have time to build them correctly."

Charlie nodded his head. He had seen the stack of wooden crates and barrels in the feed room in the barn. Maybe Grandpa would let him have a couple to play with. He and Charlotte could build a castle, or a clubhouse, or a fort, or a. . . .

"Are you ready, Freddy?" joked Grandpa, bringing Charlie's attention back to the kitchen. "You look like you were daydreaming or something. What are you thinking about?"

"Oh, just about building something," Charlie answered vaguely. He wanted to wait until they got to the barn to ask Grandpa about using the crates. First, he needed to help his grandpa with whatever chore needed to be done.

After they had solved the feeding trough problem, Charlie asked Grandpa if he could use some of the wooden crates and barrels in the barn. Grandpa told him that if he was careful, he could use some of the square ones and a couple of barrels. He showed Charlie which crates were square. This is what they looked like:

All 4 sides were the same length, and each corner was a right angle. Like this:

They looked different from the crate they had found for Pokey's bed, which looked like this:

Color the squares blue, the triangles red, the circles yellow, and the rectangles green.

There are _____ squares.

There are _____ circles.

There are _____ rectangles.

There are _____ triangles.

Today we are going to make more flashcards using these addition facts.

$$4 + 4 = 8 \qquad 5 + 5 = 10$$

Practice your addition facts using all of your flashcards.

Use your addition flashcards to drill your facts.

Practice placing the "Days of the Week" cards in order.

Numbers for copywork (say them as you write them):

10 20 30 40 50

60 70 80 90

Addition Practice

Use your counting items to solve these equations and write the answers in the blanks. Narrate to your teacher what you are doing.

$1 + 3 =$ _____

$9 + 1 =$ _____

$3 + 6 =$ _____

$5 + 3 =$ _____

$4 + 5 =$ _____

Have your student do these exercises using their 100's Chart.

1. Place a small counting item on all the 10s; explain the pattern

2. Find the number 20. What comes before? What comes after?

3. Find the number 3. What is 2 more? (Instruct your student to move his or her finger ahead 2 numbers)

4. Find the number 6. What is 4 more?

5. Find the number 5. What is 5 more?

6. Find the number 35. What comes before? What comes after?

7. Find the number 60. What comes before? What comes after?

8. Repeat with these numbers: 20, 42, 55, and 80.

9. Find the number 13. What does each digit stand for?

10. Have students narrate everything they can remember about the tens' place and the ones' place.

Say and write the numbers 20–29 from memory.

Practice your addition facts using your flashcards.

Practice your addition facts using your flashcards.

Addition practice using the + 1 pattern.

5 + 1 = _____

9 + 1 = _____

7 + 1 = _____

6 + 1 = _____

5 + 1 = _____

4 + 1 = _____

Draw a pattern using the shapes you have learned.

Review Time!

Dear Mom and Dad,

We have had a very fun week with Grandma and Grandpa. We learned a new shape! This is a square: (draw a square)

It has _____ sides, which are all the same length. It also has _____ corners, which are all right angles.

Grandpa let us use some square crates and round barrels to make a fort!

We have been learning addition facts. These are the facts we have learned so far: (Write the facts you have learned so far. You may look at your cards.)

Love, Charlotte, Charlie, and our friend _____

Two by Two (Introducing Skip Counting by 2s)

"Grandma, could you tell us a story?" Charlotte asked one afternoon. It was raining . . . again! The children were so tired of the rain. Grandpa had said at breakfast that it was a good rain, and the crops needed it. The twins were glad the crops needed it, but they missed playing with their lambs outside. Today, Grandma had asked them to help fold laundry. She had decided that since there was no sign of the rain letting up, she would go ahead and use her clothes dryer. The laundry needed to be done!

"What story would you like to hear, Charlotte?" Grandma asked. Charlotte shrugged. She wasn't sure, but Grandma always had good stories. Grandma's eyes twinkled, "How would you two like to hear a story about a rain storm that lasted 40 days and forty nights? That's 4 groups of 10!

Like this:

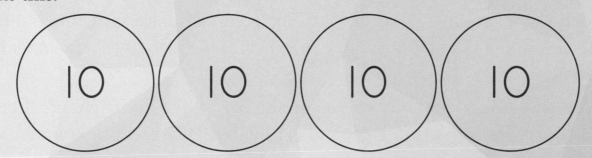

That's 40 days! This story happened long ago. In fact it happened so long ago, that it's in the Bible."

The children stopped matching socks and looked at Grandma with their mouths open. Was she kidding? Grandma was known for her practical jokes, but this time, she seemed serious. A rainstorm that lasted 40 days and nights? "Yes, Grandma! Tell us. Tell us, please!"

Grandma chuckled, "Okay! Like I said, this story is in the Bible. So that makes it 100 percent true. The Bible is the only book in the world that we can completely trust. Always remember that, children.

Okay, this story is called 'Noah's Ark,' and it happened thousands of years ago. That's many, many groups of 10!

"A long, long time ago, the earth was very full of bad people who did bad things. This made God very sad, and it also made Him very angry. He became so sad and angry that He wished He had never made man to live on the earth. It seemed like everyone was bad! But He knew of one man who was not bad. This man's name was Noah, and he lived his life to please God.

"God decided to use a great flood to wash away all the bad people who refused to listen to Him. But He wanted Noah and his family to be safe, so He told Noah to build a huge boat. This wasn't like any boat you children have ever seen! Noah's ark was more like a huge, floating box. God told Noah just how big to make the Ark, and what materials to use.

"Noah was a good man, and he was obedient to God. He started to build the Ark. It took him 150 years to build it. People in Bible days lived a lot longer than they do now!

"Every day, he and his sons worked on the Ark. All of his neighbors thought he was crazy. They came and made fun of him, but Noah kept right on building.

He knew what God was going to do. He also knew that God was going to use this huge boat to save him and his family. God had told him to gather food for the animals that He was also going to save on the Ark.

"As he built, Noah warned and pleaded with his neighbors and friends to listen to him. He tried to tell them that God was sending a huge flood. Nobody had ever seen a flood before, so they didn't believe Noah. How sad Noah was that nobody would listen! He knew that all of these people were going to die.

"One day the ark was finished, and Noah and his family were ready to move on board. The door of the huge boat was open, for it was too heavy for Noah and his sons to close. The people laughed at Noah some more. They thought he had made a mistake when he made the door so big. But Noah had not made a mistake, for he had followed God's plans for the Ark. Out of the woods, deserts, and swamps came animals. How did they know to come? Noah and his sons did not have to go get them. No! God sent them. There were two of every kind of creature! From deer to dinosaurs, from chipmunks to alligators . . . they all came. There was a line of animals as far as you could see! Two by two, they came marching peacefully into the Ark. Animals that usually would be afraid of humans came in. Lions fell into step behind the gazelles.

"Can you imagine what it would be like to see such a thing? Only God could have done this! And remember the door? After the last animal had fled into the Ark, God closed the door. Just like that, the enormous door creaked closed with a final boom! Soon, it started to rain. It rained harder than we have ever seen it rain. In fact, it rained in sheets and buckets of water. God caused the waters under the ground to come up, breaking through the earth's crust.

"Soon, everything outside the ark had been swept away in the water. Can you imagine how bumpy that ride was? All those animals were safely in the Ark along with Noah, his wife, their sons and their daughters-in-law. God must have made the animals sleepy or calm for them to be in the Ark so long. After 40 days and nights, it finally stopped raining, but the water was still everywhere!

"After a very long time on the Ark, Noah sent out a raven and a dove. The dove came back because it could not find a place to land. Noah waited a week, and then sent the dove back out. This time the dove returned with an olive branch in its beak. Again Noah sent out the dove, and this time, it did not return. He knew that there must be dry land!

"Noah's family had been on the ark for over a year when finally the water had receded enough for them to leave the Ark. The boat had come to rest on a mountain, and so Noah and his family stepped out on dry land. As they stood and worshipped God for saving them, they looked up to see a beautiful rainbow across the sky. God told them that whenever they saw a rainbow again, to remember His promise that He would never again use a flood to destroy the earth."

The animals came into the ark 2 by 2. We can count using 2s. Trace the numbers and fill in the missing numbers, saying them out loud as you write them.

The numbers that you filled in are the numbers we use when we count by 2s.

Addition Practice

Use small counting items to solve these equations. Narrate to your teacher what you are doing. Write the answers in the blanks.

$3 + 3 =$ _____ $2 + 5 =$ _____

$8 + 1 =$ _____ $2 + 3 =$ _____

$7 + 2 =$ _____ $6 + 4 =$ _____

Use your flashcards to practice your addition facts.

Practice counting by 2s. Use small counting items, or if you have them, small toy animals. Line them up 2 by 2 like the animals going into Noah's ark. Count out loud and then use the numbers as copywork.

0   2   4   6   8   10

Use your flashcards to practice your addition facts.

Finish the pattern by coloring what comes next.

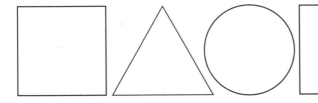

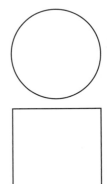

Practice putting the "Days of the Week" cards in order.

Using your 100's Chart, place a small counting item, such as a button or bean, on each number you say when you count by 2s. Do you see the pattern? Discuss the pattern you see. Continue counting by 2s up to 20. Look at the last digit of each number, and write the pattern on the lines below. The first 2 are done for you.

0 , 2 , _____ ; _____ ;

_____ , 10 , 12 , _____ ;

_____ ; _____ ; _____

Count the objects and write the correct number.

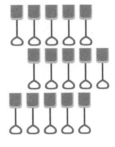

27 _____   9 _____   15 _____

6 _____   15 _____   12 _____

Numbers for copywork. Say the numbers as you write them. Narrate to your teacher about the pattern you see.

0   2   4   6   8   10

12   14   16   18   20

Practice putting your "Days of the Week" cards in order. Trace the days of the week.

Sunday   Monday

Tuesday   Wednesday

Thursday   Friday

Saturday

There are _____ days in a week.

Review Time!

> **Teacher**
>
> *Today you are going to let your student show what they have learned this week. Have them use their 100's Chart and counters to narrate what they have learned about counting by 2s up to 20. To learn more about show and tells and oral presentations consult teaching companion.*

On the lines below, take notes on how they are doing. Are there areas that need to be reviewed?

After they have explained the concept of 2s, let them retell the story of Noah's ark. You may choose to have them do it orally (this might be fun using small animals and a box to represent the Ark), or they may draw a picture of it on a separate piece of paper. Either way, encourage them to show the animals coming to the Ark, 2 by 2.

Teacher's notes: Date: _____

_____

_____

_____

_____

_____

_____

_____

_____

Please read Genesis 7:2–3 to see exactly how many of each kind of animal were sent to the Ark. For the sake of the lesson about counting by 2s, I focus on those animals that were sent in pairs.

Number Families, Addition to Ten

"Could you show us more about numbers, Grandpa?" Charlotte asked one evening around a mouthful of mashed potatoes. The twins had been playing with Ann and Andy all day. The lambs were getting bigger and stronger every day! Grandpa had told them that morning, that by the end of the summer, the lambs would be as big as the children.

"What would you like to know, Charlotte?" Grandpa replied after wiping some stray potatoes off of her chin. "Please don't talk with food in your mouth, Sugar-pots," he admonished her.

"I'm sorry, Grandpa. I want to know how numbers go together. I know that when you add two numbers together, you come up with a bigger number, but what else do they do?" Charlotte wanted to know.

"Well, did you know that there are 'families' of numbers?" Grandpa asked the children. "I'll show you after we are done eating and helping Grandma with the supper dishes, okay?" The children nodded their heads together.

After the supper dishes had been dried and put away, Grandpa invited the twins to come into the family room. They knelt together by the coffee table, and after moving their Place Value Village to the side, Grandpa poured out a pile of dried beans. The children watched intently as Grandpa's big, work-worn hands counted out four dried beans and lined them up carefully in front of the children.

179

"How many beans have I lined up, children?" he asked.

"Four, Grandpa!" they said together.

"That's right," Grandpa took two more beans out of the pile and placed them near the other four. "Now how many do we have all together?" he asked the children.

"One, two, three, four, five, six. Six! There are six all together," Charlotte answered.

"That's right. Now, I want you to watch carefully," Grandpa instructed as he moved one of the two beans over to join the four beans. "Now we have five beans here, and only one over here. Do we still have six beans?" The children looked at the beans carefully. There were still six beans. They nodded. Grandpa continued to move the beans around. Each combination he made, added up to six. Like this:

4 beans + 2 beans = 6 beans

1 bean + 5 beans = 6 beans

3 beans + 3 beans = 6 beans

2 beans + 4 beans = 6 beans

5 beans + 1 bean = 6 beans

"You see, children, all of these numbers make up the 6 family! Now you try it!"

Let's find all the "members" of the "10's family." Start by taking out 10 counting items; beans would be best. As you play with the beans, tell your teacher the different combinations which make up 10. The first two are done for you.

$9 + 1 = 10$ ____ + ____ = 10

$1 + 9 = 10$ ____ + ____ = 10

____ + ____ = 10 ____ + ____ = 10

____ + ____ = 10 ____ + ____ = 10

____ + ____ = 10 ____ + ____ = 10

What are the "members" in the 10's family?

Use your flashcards to review your math facts.

Numbers for copywork (say them as you write them):

0 2 4 6 8 10

12 14 16 18 20

Using your 100's Chart and small counting items, practice counting by 2s up to 20.

Write the numbers for copywork (say the numbers as you write them):

O 2 4 6 8 10

12 14 16 18 20

Use your Addition Mat (horizontal) and small counting items to solve these addition equations. Consider writing them on your Addition Mat (vertical) as well. Narrate to your teacher as you work. Write the answer in the blanks.

9 + 1 = _10_   6 + 4 = _10_

8 + 2 = _10_   2 + 8 = _10_

7 + 3 = _10_   5 + 5 = _10_

Today, you are going to make flashcards for the "10's family." Draw pictures to show the facts.

Use your Place Value Village and Place Value Village Counting Mat to count out 45 items.

How many groups of 10? _____

How many groups of 1? _____

Write the number: _____

Write the numbers that you say when you count to 20 by 2s.

_____

- -

_____

_____

- -

_____

Using red, yellow, blue, and green construction paper (or 4 other colors — one for each shape), cut and glue squares, rectangles, triangles, and circles into a picture. Explain the pattern to your teacher.

Using the flashcards that you made yesterday, practice your 10's family addition facts.

Numbers for copywork (Say the numbers as you write them.):

50 51 52 53 54

55 56 57 58 59

Show your teacher these numbers on your 100's Chart.

Review Time! Today, you are going to help the children write a letter to their parents.

Dear Mom and Dad,

We can't wait to show you what we have learned this week. Grandpa showed us that numbers have families! We learned all the numbers that are in the 10's family, like this:

_____ + _____ = 10   _____ + _____ = 10

_____ + _____ = 10   _____ + _____ = 10

_____ + _____ = 10   _____ + _____ = 10

_____ + _____ = 10   _____ + _____ = 10

_____ + _____ = 10   _____ + _____ = 10

We also can write these numbers. Write the numbers we say when we count by 2s, 0–20.

_____

_____

_____

_____

Love, Charlotte, Charlie and our friend _____

Practice your math facts using the flashcards you have made so far. Are you starting to remember them? Are there certain ones you have a harder time remembering? Write them in the space below and spend a few extra minutes studying them.

Math facts I need to study:

In our next lesson, we are going to be learning about another pattern in nature. Students will be sprouting a bean. Every day they will be observing it and recording their observations. Please make sure you have the following items in preparation.

1. glass jar

2. white paper towel

3. a good, healthy dried bean

Counting by 10

Kerplink . . . kerplunk . . . kerplink. . . . Charlotte loved the sound of the peas hitting the metal bowl in her lap. She had gotten to do so many fun things since coming to her grandparents' farm! She smiled, remembering the first time she had helped Grandpa milk Bossy the cow. Charlotte had been just a little nervous about trying it, but with Grandpa's help, she had filled up a small pail that she had proudly brought to Grandma in the kitchen.

Her days had been filled with new experiences, that was for sure, and this was another one! She and Charlie were helping Grandma shell peas for supper. They had picked them earlier in the afternoon, and now the three of them sat on the screened-in kitchen porch, with the basket between them.

"Children, did you know that we actually eat the seed part of a pea plant?" Grandma asked. "These little sweet peas are actually what we plant in the spring to grow the big pea plant."

"It's another pattern, isn't it, Grandma?" Charlie asked. He held up a pea and looked at it carefully. It was hard to imagine a whole big pea plant coming from this little pea! "Wait a minute! Grandma, this one is broken! See? It has a crack!" Charlie exclaimed, showing her the pea in his hand.

"No, Charlie, that is the way they all are," Grandma explained with a smile. "Look, they all have that little crack." The children dipped their hands down into the shelled peas in their bowls.

"Look! They do have cracks . . . all of them! Why? Why do they have cracks?" Charlotte wanted to know. Grandma carefully slipped her thumbnail into the crack of a pea, and to the amazement of the children, it fell into two pieces in her hand.

"Look, do you see this tiny, little leaf?" Grandma asked the children. They came and peered into her hand.

"Yes! I see it! Do you, Charlie?" Charlotte squealed. Charlie nodded his head.

"Why is there a tiny plant in there, Grandma?" he asked.

"Well, when you plant the seed, which is one of these peas, this part of the seed becomes food for this little baby plant. This tiny part becomes the root, and this part becomes the stem. Would you two like to do an experiment?" Grandma smiled at the children.

"What kind of experiment?" the children wanted to know.

"You know those dried beans that Grandpa uses to teach you about numbers? They are like these peas; they are seeds and have a little plant inside of them. I can show you how to sprout one. In just a few days, you can have a bean that has a stem and a root! Would you like to do that?"

The children's eyes were big, and they nodded in excitement. "Can we do it now, Grandma? Please? Please?" they jumped up and down. Grandma smiled at their excitement.

"Well, let's wait until after supper, and I will show you how. Can you help me finish these peas, so I can get dinner on the table?" Grandma answered.

See Bean Sprouting Project Instructions in the Appendix.

When we have a large number of items to count, it makes it easier to count by groups of 10. Take out your 100's Chart and point to these numbers. After you say them, copy them.

10 20 30 40 50

60 70 80 90 100

Narrate to your teacher what the first digit in these numbers stands for (groups of ten). Narrate what the second digit stands for (groups of one).

Look at the number 100. How many digits does it have? We can see that it has a 10 in the tens' place, and a 0 in the ones' place: 100. When we have 100 items, we have 10 groups of 10. Look at your Place Value Village. How many groups can live in the TENS' house? That means we have to "bundle up" the 10 groups of 10, and move them next door to the HUNDREDS' house.

HUNDREDS' house	TENS' house	ONES' house
1	0	0

There is one group of 100 and zero groups of 10s and 1s. Practice counting 100 items using your Place Value Village. Narrate to your teacher while you count.

Draw a picture of what your bean looks like.

Day 1

Using your 100's Chart, practice counting by 10s.

Numbers for copywork (say the numbers as you write them):

10   20   30   40   50

60   70   80   90   100

Narrate to your teacher what each digit stands for.

Addition Practice

3 + 3 = _____   2 + 4 = _____

5 + 1 = _____   5 + 3 = _____

7 + 2 = _____   4 + 5 = _____

Carefully observe your bean. Draw what you see.

Day 2

Use your flashcards to practice your math facts.

Trace the numbers, filling in the missing numbers, counting by 10s.

_____,  , _____, _____,

_____, 60, 70,  , _____,

 , _____

Practice counting the groups by 10.

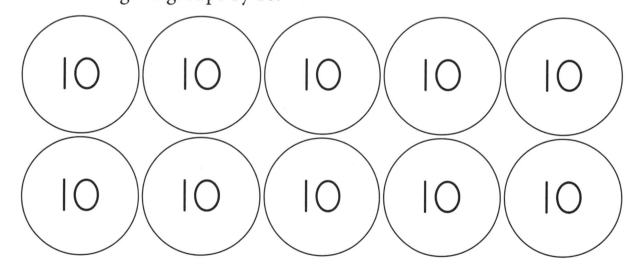

Carefully observe your bean. Draw what you see.

Day 3

Numbers to write. Write the numbers you say when you count by 10s to 100.

_____

- -

_____

_____

- -

_____

Find the numbers on your 100's Chart.

Use your Place Value Village Counting Mat to count out 50 items. Do not erase the numbers you write; we will be using them in tomorrow's lesson.

Carefully observe your bean. Draw what you see.

Day 4

Use your flashcards to practice your math facts.

Review Time!

Use your Place Value Village and Place Value Village Counting Mat to count out 50 more items, bringing the number up to 100.

How many groups of 100 do you have? _____

How many groups of 10 do you have? _____

How many groups of 1 do you have? _____

Write the number _____.

Use your number cards 0–9, your Addition Mat (horizontal), and small counting items to practice addition. Consider writing them on your Addition Mat (vertical) as well. Narrate to your teacher what you are doing. Write some of your addition equations.

My addition equations:

Carefully observe your bean. Draw what you see.

Day 5

If you would like to continue observing your bean, here are three more spaces to record what you see.

Day _____

Day _____

Day _____

Counting Groups

"Grandpa, I'm getting better at casting! Look, I got my line way out there!" Charlie looked proud of himself. When he and Charlotte had first come to the farm, he couldn't get the fishing pole to cooperate at all! Now, with just a little help from Grandpa, he was catching at least one fish every time they went to the fishing hole.

"You are doing much better, Charlie! In fact, you two may come to the fishing hole by yourselves from now on, if you would like." Grandpa scratched his head, then added, "But you better wear life jackets to be on the safe side, okay?" The children nodded.

"Grandpa, how are fish born? How can a mommy fish have a baby when she is in the water?" Charlotte had become extremely interested in baby animals since Grandpa had given them Ann and Andy. She was always wanting to know about every creature.

"Well, Charlotte, the mommy fish does have her babies in the water." When he saw the surprised look on her face, he added, "They are not like chicken eggs though. Actually, fish lay hundreds of eggs at one time. The cluster of eggs stick together while the fish inside forms. Pretty soon, the fish hatch out of the eggs and are able to swim around." The children looked at each other in amazement. Imagine hundreds of eggs!

"Grandpa, how do you count hundreds of baby fish? How does the mommy fish know they are hers? Does she take care of them?" Charlie had a lot of questions.

"My goodness! One question at a time!" Grandpa chuckled, "First, after the mommy fish lays the eggs, she really doesn't do anything. Most kinds of fish just swim off and the eggs are on their own. Second, you can count groups of 100 just like you do groups of 10.

"There are 3 groups of 100, so you count like this, 'One hundred, two hundred, three hundred.' Remember, 100 is 10 groups of 10."

$$\left(\,100\,\right)\left(\,100\,\right)\left(\,100\,\right)$$

In our last lesson, we learned how to count by 10s. Using your 100's Chart, say the numbers out loud as you point to the numbers, and then copy them.

10 20 30 40 50

------

60 70 80 90 100

Today, we learned we can count big numbers by counting groups of 100. Practice counting these groups of 100.

In the space below, draw and color a pattern, using circles, triangles, squares, and rectangles. Explain your pattern to your teacher.

My shape pattern:

Addition Practice

Use small counting items to solve these equations.

$4 + 3 =$ _____ $2 + 5 =$ _____

$8 + 1 =$ _____ $5 + 3 =$ _____

$6 + 2 =$ _____ $4 + 4 =$ _____

Numbers for copywork (say the numbers as you write them):

30 31 32 33 34

35 36 37 38 39

Use small counting items or small toy animals to practice counting by 2s up to 20. Point to the numbers on your 100's Chart as you say them.

Practice your addition facts with your flashcards.

Color all the squares red, all the rectangles green, all the circles orange, and all the triangles yellow.

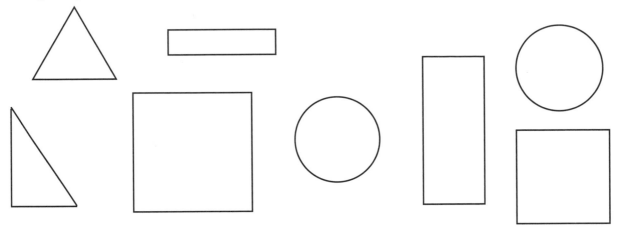

How many squares? _____   How many rectangles? _____

How many circles? _____   How many triangles? _____

Numbers for copywork (say the numbers as you write them):

40 41 42 43 44

45 46 47 48 49

Show your teacher these numbers on your 100's Chart.

Carefully count and write how many are in each set.

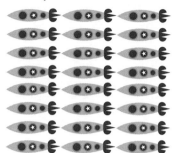

_____

_____

_____

_____

_____

_____

Use your Place Value Village and Place Value Village Counting Mat to count 35 objects. Narrate to your teacher what you are doing.

How many groups of 10 do you have? _____

How many groups of 1? _____

Write the number _____

Practice your addition facts using your flashcards.

Review Time! Grandpa drew this picture of a fish life cycle for the children. Take time to color it and talk about the life cycle patterns we have learned about so far.

 eggs

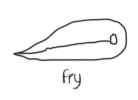 fry

 adult

Practice counting by 2s. Say, trace, and write the numbers.

 , _2_,  , _6_, _8_, _____,

_____, _14_, _____, _18_, _20_

Count by 10s. Say, trace, and write the numbers.

_____, _____, _20_, _30_,

_____, _____, _____, _70_,

_80_, _____, _____

On your 100's Chart, find the numbers that you wrote above. Practice counting groups of 100.

(100) (100) (100) (100) (100)

Solving for an Unknown

"Be careful, Charlie, don't bump my elbow!" Charlotte exclaimed as she carefully scooped cornmeal with a measuring cup. The twins had brought the fish they had caught up to the house. Grandma had deemed them the "best looking sunnies" she had ever seen. And there were five of them, which were enough for dinner.

"They'll be delicious with the fresh broccoli, yellow squash, and tomatoes that I'm preparing for dinner! Mmm, mmm! Yes, children, you two have provided dinner for all of us. You should be mighty proud of yourselves! I'll even show you how to fry them. A little egg, cornmeal and seasonings. . . . They'll be the best fish you ever tasted!"

"How many cups of this do I need, Grandma?" Charlotte asked wiping her hands on her apron, leaving yellow streaks down her sides. Cooking was messy work!

"Well, how many do you have so far?" Grandma came to look over Charlotte's shoulder. "We need four cups all together."

"I put one in so far," Charlotte answered. "So how many more do I need?"

"Let's figure it out . . . you have 1 + _____ = 4," Grandma wrote on a scrap of paper. Charlotte looked at her fingers, "Hmmm. I have 1." She held up one finger. "And 2 comes after 1, so 2, 3, 4. I counted 3 more fingers. Is that right, Grandma?"

"Yes, Charlotte that is right. Good job! What you just did is what we call 'solving for an unknown.' When you know how much you need all together, you can figure out how much more you need by counting up, just like you did."

$$3 + \_\_\_\_\_ = 5$$

You can see by comparing the 3 objects to the 5 objects, that the missing number is 2. Practice this concept with beans. Practice counting up from a smaller number to a larger number.

Let's practice solving for an unknown. It is very important to use counting items to learn this concept.

Place 2 counting items on the table. How many more items do we need to have 4?

_____

Place 3 counting items on the table. How many more items do we need to have 6?

_____

Place 1 counting item on the table. How many more items do we need to have 5?

_____

Place 4 counting items on the table. How many more items do we need to have 8?

_____

Place 5 counting items on the table. How many more items do we need to have 10?

_____

Numbers for copywork: (Say the numbers as you write them. Find them on your 100's Chart)

10 11 12 13 14 15

Practice solving for an unknown. Remember to use your counting items! Narrate to your teacher what you are doing. This time have your teacher help you write an addition equation to show what you did. The first one is done for you.

Place 4 counting items on the table. How many more items do we need to have 7?

___3___ $4 + 3 = 7$

Place 2 counting items on the table. How many more items do we need to have 6?

_____

Place 1 counting item on the table. How many more items do we need to have 8?

_____

Place 5 counting items on the table. How many more items do we need to have 9?

_____

Place 6 counting items on the table. How many more items do we need to have 10?

_____

Numbers for copywork. Say them as you write them. Find them on your 100's Chart.

16 17 18 19 20

Practice solving for an unknown. Remember to use your counting items!

Narrate to your teacher what you are doing. Write an addition equation to show what you did.

Place 2 counting items on the table. How many more items do we need to have 10?

_____

Place 6 counting items on the table. How many more items do we need to have 7?

_____

Place 1 counting item on the table. How many more items do we need to have 5?

_____

Place 5 counting items on the table. How many more items do we need to have 8?

_____

Place 3 counting items on the table. How many more items do we need to have 10?

_____

Practice counting by 10 from 10–100. Find them on your 100's Chart. Write the numbers.

_____

- -

_____

- -

_____

Now it's your turn! Using your Addition Mat (horizontal), number cards (0–10), and counting items, make up your own "solve for an unknown" equations.
Like this:

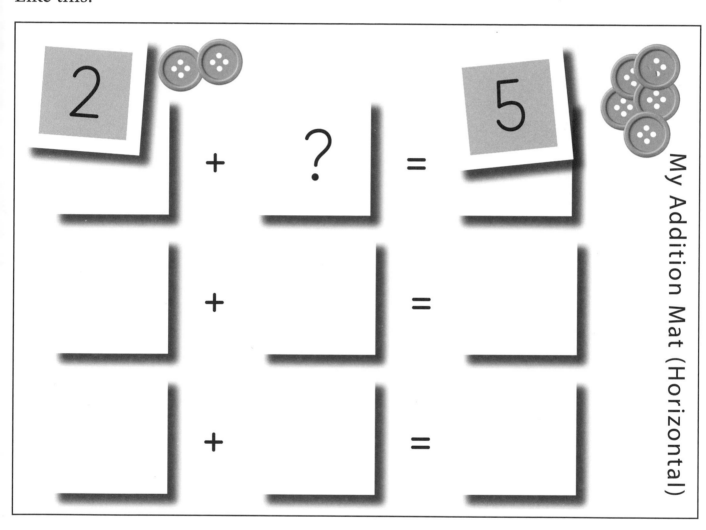

Using your Place Value Village, count out 60 items. Narrate what you are doing.

How many groups of 10? _____

How many groups of 1? _____

Use your flashcards to practice your math facts.

Review time! Help the twins write a letter to their parents showing what you have learned this week.

Dear Mom and Dad,

We have had such an exciting week! Grandma taught us something new, and we want to show you. (Use your counting items to solve these equations.)

$4 + 3 =$ _____ $2 + 5 =$ _____

$8 + 1 =$ _____ $5 + 3 =$ _____

$6 + 2 =$ _____ $4 + 4 =$ _____

We also learned how to count groups of 100, (practice counting groups of 100).

and we can write the numbers, counting by 2s to 20!

_____

- -

_____

- -

_____

Love, Charlotte, Charlie and our friend _____

Tally Marks to Make Groups of Five

"Children, I could really use your help this morning. I need to fill some special orders for some of my customers. This afternoon is farmers' market, and I need to deliver these orders. Do you think you can help me?" Grandpa asked the children at breakfast one morning.

"We can help, Grandpa. May we go with you to the farmers' market? Please? We will be very good, and we are big helpers!" Both the twins were pleading now. Grandpa smiled at the twins and looked over their heads at Grandma.

"It's alright with me, if it's alright with Grandma! If she doesn't need you for anything," Grandpa said.

"No, they can go with you, Honey. All I'm doing this afternoon is cleaning out the fridge. You children don't want to help me with that chore, do you?" Grandma had a twinkle in her eye.

"No! We would rather go with Grandpa!" they said together.

"Okay, but first we have work to do. I have five orders I need to fill. We will have to harvest, wash, and pack these first, okay? You two need to find a piece of paper and a pencil. I'm going to show you how to make tally marks to help us count," Grandpa instructed the children. The children ran to obey, and soon they came back with a notepad and pencil.

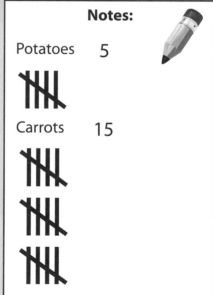

As Grandpa carefully harvested the carrots, beets, and potatoes, Charlie placed them in the wheelbarrow. Charlotte did as Grandpa directed her to. This is what she wrote: ⟶

Grandpa had shown her how to make 1 tally mark for every carrot or potato. When she had reached 4 tally marks, the fifth one went across the group. This made nice and neat little groups of 5. Charlotte liked doing tally marks!

"Okay, Children, I think that just about does it!" Grandpa said as he loaded the last box of veggies into the back of his truck. "You two go wash your hands and faces, and ask Grandma if she thinks you need to put cleaner clothes on. I'll wait for you, but try to be quick, okay?"

The children nodded and ran up to the house. Within a few minutes, they came skipping back with clean hands, faces, and clothes. Grandma had helped them to change quickly. They chattered excitedly about their trip to the farmers' market as they clambered up into the pickup truck. Grandpa smiled as he reminded them to buckle up their seat belts, and off they went!

"Grandpa, how far is it to town?" Charlie wanted to know. He hoped it was a long drive, because he loved to ride in the pickup truck.

"It's 15 miles," Grandpa chuckled at Charlie's enthusiasm. His grandson's energy amazed him!

"That would be 3 groups of tally marks, right Grandpa?" Charlotte asked after counting on her fingers.

"Yes, it would, Charlotte. Good job!" Grandpa was pleased at how well Charlotte had understood tally marks. "Pretty soon I will teach you both how to count by 5s! It makes counting a lot easier and faster."

Let's practice making tally marks. Count each item and make 1 tally mark. Remember, Grandpa showed Charlotte that the fifth mark goes across the other 4. The first one is done for you.

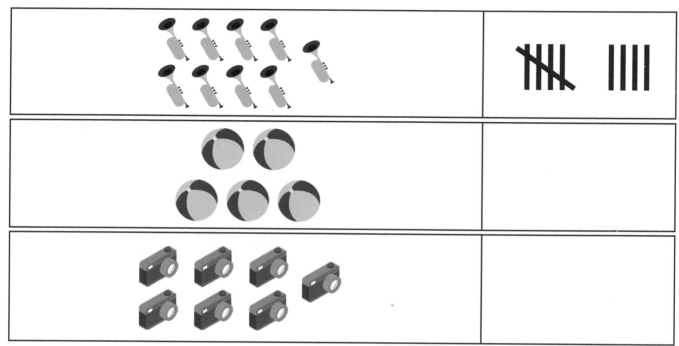

Numbers for copywork. Say them as you write them, then find them on your 100's Chart.

10 20 30 40 50

60 70 80 90 100

Count the tally marks. Draw pictures and the number to match in the rectangles below. The first one is done for you.

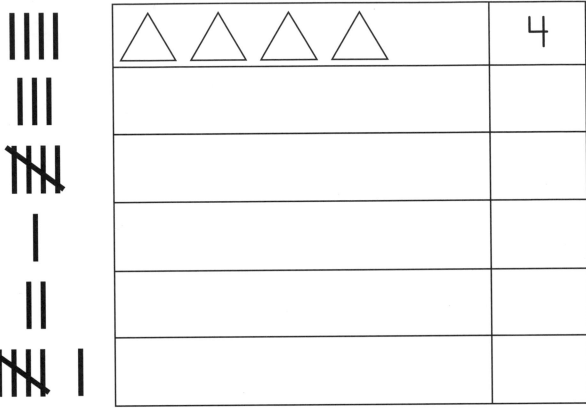

Fill in the missing parts. Finish the words to show the days of the week. Sing the song if you need to.

_____ day

_____ day

_____ day

_____ day

_____ day

_____ day

_____ day

There are _____ days in a week.

Make tally marks and write the number.

_____ _____   _____ _____   _____ _____

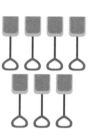

_____ _____   _____ _____   _____ _____

Addition Practice

Use counting items to solve these equations. Remember to narrate to your teacher, explaining what you are doing.

$4 + 3 =$ _____ $2 + 5 =$ _____

$8 + 1 =$ _____ $5 + 3 =$ _____

$6 + 2 =$ _____ $4 + 4 =$ _____

Match the tally marks to the right group of objects.

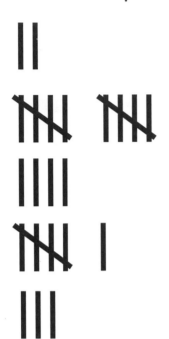 

Numbers for copywork. Say the words as you write them, then find them on your 100's Chart.

40 41 42 43 44

45 46 47 48 49

Review Time!

Today, you are going to do an oral presentation about what you have been learning. Let's have fun with this! If you have poster board, use a piece or two to make posters of what you have learned. You could draw pictures or use stickers for objects and then write tally marks next to them. You can set up a display, using your Addition Mat and small counting items. Use your display to show how you can solve for an unknown. Decorate and have fun doing your show and tell!

Some other ideas:

- Bake a special desert, helping your teacher to measure and count!

- Cut out pictures of different life cycles/patterns that you have learned about.

- Challenge someone else to solve an addition equation you make up.

- Go on a scavenger hunt to find shapes, numbers, and patterns. Invite your class or family to help you count using tally marks.

Teacher

Take note of how well your student is showing mastery of concepts.

Teacher's notes:

_____
_____
_____
_____
_____
_____
_____
_____

Solve for the unknown number.

② + ? = ⑤

? + ③ = ⑧

? + ② = ④

? + ① = ⑥

⑥ + ? = ⑫

⓪ ① ② ③ ④ ⑤ ⑥ ⑦ ⑧ ⑨ + −
⑩ ⑪ ⑫ ⑬ ⑭ ⑮ ⑯ ⑰ ⑱ ⑲ ⑳ =
0 1 2 3 4 5 6 7 8 9 + − =

Counting by 5s

The days were getting shorter, and the wind carried a faint hint of the coming fall. Summer was almost over, and along with it, the twins' visit to the farm. Soon they would be saying goodbye to Grandma and Grandpa and returning to their own home. They were happy and sad at the same time.

They had seen Mom and Dad only two times during their visit to the farm, when they had come on a couple of weekends to see the children. On their last visit, Mom and Dad had told the children all about the mission's trip they had gone on. They had been in South America for over a month, helping to rebuild an orphanage that had been destroyed by a flood. Their story had reminded the children of the story of Noah's ark.

Charlie and Charlotte missed their parents but understood that being with Grandma and Grandpa was the next best thing. They had learned so much, and they knew that they would miss their grandparents very much when they returned to their home. On one of their parents' visits, Mom had told them a very happy secret. The twins were going to be a big brother and sister; Mom was having a baby! She told them that the baby was going to be born right around Christmas.

The children didn't want to waste a single minute of the rest of their visit. They were very busy helping Grandpa harvest the vegetables. Once in a while, they even helped with the barn chores when Grandpa was too busy to do it all. Late summer is a busy, busy time when you live on a farm! The children were so tired by supper that they could hardly stay awake to eat.

Just like everything else on the farm, harvest time was done in an orderly way. Grandpa showed the children how to bundle everything in groups of 5. He said it was much easier to pack into crates and boxes to take to the farmers' market. He taught the children how to count by 5s and then write the number on the label of the boxes. It's really quite easy to count by 5s, because every number you say ends in a "0" or a "5."

Like this:

0, 5, 10, 15, 20, 25 . . .

Do you see how every other number ends in 0, and the numbers in between end in 5? It's a pattern.

You try it now! Trace the numbers and say them out loud. Find them on your 100's Chart.

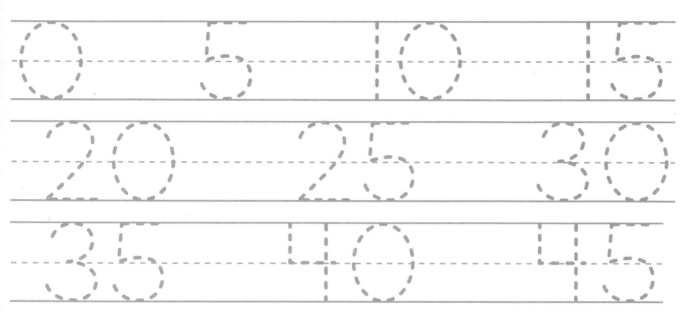

Place a small counting item on each number as you say it. Talk about the pattern you see.

Addition. Solving for an unknown. Use your counting items to solve these equations.

4 + _____ = 6   2 + _____ = 10

8 + _____ = 9   5 + _____ = 7

6 + _____ = 8   3 + _____ = 9

Trace the numbers below. Fill in the missing numbers in the counting by 5s pattern. Say the numbers out loud as you write them.

_____ , _____

Now let's trace the next 5 numbers in the pattern.

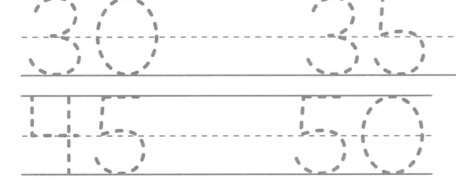

Find all of the numbers above on your 100's Chart. Narrate the pattern you see. What does each number end in?

_____ and _____

Using all the shapes you have learned, draw and color a pattern in the space below. Explain the pattern to your teacher.

My pattern:

Numbers for copywork. Say the numbers as you write them, and find them on your 100's Chart.

Addition practice. Solve for the unknown.

6 + _____ = 10   3 + _____ = 6

4 + _____ = 9   2 + _____ = 8

6 + _____ = 9   5 + _____ = 7

Use your Place Value Village and Place Value Village Counting Mat to count out 45 items.

How many groups of 10? _____

How many groups of 1? _____

Match the tally mark with the numbers.

卌		4
					6
卌 卌	8
卌 |||	3
卌	2
			10
		7
卌 ||	9
卌 ||||	5
				1

Numbers for copywork. Find them on your 100's Chart.

0 2 4 6 8 10

_____

- -

_____

What pattern is this? Counting by _____.

Review Time! Help the children write a letter home to their parents.

Dear Mom and Dad,

How are you doing? We want to show you what we can do.

Count by 2s to 20.

_____

- -

_____

_____

- -

_____

Trace the numbers below, then fill in the missing numbers, counting by 5s to 50.

0, _____, _____,

15, 20, _____,

_____, 35, _____,

_____, 50,

We have been having fun with tally marks too! Tally marks are like counting by 5s, because they are in groups of 5!

(Draw pictures for each group of tally marks and write the number in the rectangles below.)

Love, Charlie, Charlotte, and our friend, _____

Teacher *Gather these items for our next lesson: 1 brass fastener, contact paper.*

Telling Time, Part 1

"Ding!" The kitchen timer was notifying Grandma that her biscuits were finished. Grabbing a hot pad, she deftly removed the pan from the oven, and slid the biscuits onto the cooling rack. The children watched as she flicked open a clean, white dishcloth and covered the biscuits with it. "Why do you do that, Grandma?" Charlotte inquired. "Why do the biscuits need to be covered?" "I want to make sure there are no nasty flies walking all over them, that's why," Grandma replied. She despised the flies at this time of year. It seemed like they came in through the walls. "Oh, what pests!" she would exclaim while stalking around brandishing the fly swatter like a deadly weapon.

The children looked at each other and smiled. Grandma always got the funniest look on her face when she talked about the flies. "I'm starving! What time is supper, anyway?" Charlie asked.

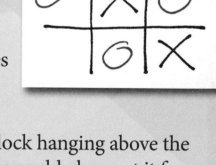

"Dinner will be ready in about 50 minutes, children. Meanwhile, why don't you two go wash up your hands and faces. You have just enough time to color a picture or play some tic-tac-toe before setting the table. We don't want the plates on the table too early, you know! Those filthy flies. . . ." The children glanced at each other; the flies again. They ran to wash their hands.

"Grandma, how long is 50 minutes? Is it an hour? Is it more than an hour?" Charlotte stared at the big kitchen clock hanging above the stove. It was always a mystery to her how her grandparents could glance at it for just a second and say what time it was! "Can you show Charlie and me how to tell time like that?" Charlotte had begged Grandma on more than one occasion.

Grandma wiped her hands on her apron and sat down next to her grandchildren. "Do you two know how many minutes are in one hour?" she asked them. When they shook their heads, she took a piece of their paper and an orange crayon. "There are 60 minutes in one hour. Here, children, take a look at this. It is very important to learn to tell time in stages." Grandma drew a circle with the orange crayon. "Let's pretend that this circle is the face of the kitchen clock, okay?" The children nodded their heads together.

"As you can see, the clock has numbers on it. The number 12 is at the very top; then the other numbers go like this." Grandma quickly wrote the numbers 1–11 around the rest of the clock. "Do you see how there are little marks between the numbers? Look closely." The twins squinted as they looked at the clock. Yes! They did see the little marks. "Those little marks are minutes. So, there are 5 minutes between each of the big numbers. Remember how Grandpa has been teaching you to count by 5s? Well, that's how you count the minutes on a clock. So let's count the minutes together. Starting at the top, we go to the right. Every number stands for 5 minutes. Like this:

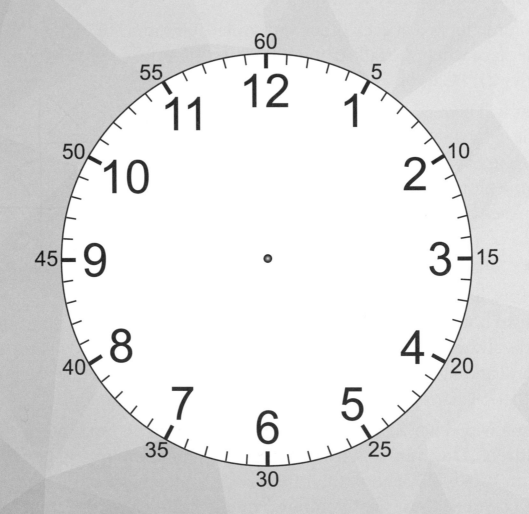

"By counting by 5s, we can see that there are 60 minutes in an hour."

Math Level 1 – Lesson 24

Now you try it! We have
learned how to count to 50
by 5s. Fill in those numbers
on the clock. Some of them
are done for you.

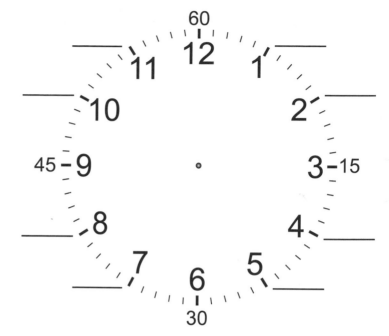

This is the first step in learning how to tell time! Remember, when counting
minutes, always start at the top and move to the right.

Numbers to write. Write the numbers you say when you count by 5s from 0–50.
Find them on the 100's chart.

_____

- -

_____

_____

- -

_____

Addition practice. Using your Addition Mat (horizontal), number cards 0–10,
and small counting items, make up 5 addition equations. Narrate to your teacher
what you are doing.

Make 2 new flashcards with these 2 addition facts:

$$3 + 4 = 7 \quad \text{and} \quad 4 + 5 = 9$$

Today you will assemble your own clock. You will find it in the back of this book on page 341. Follow the directions carefully!

Now use your clock to practice counting minutes by 5s.

Make tally marks for each set of pictures.

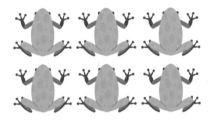

_____

_____

_____

_____

_____

_____

Using your flashcards, practice your math facts.

Practice counting by 5s using your clock. Fill in the hours on this clock face.

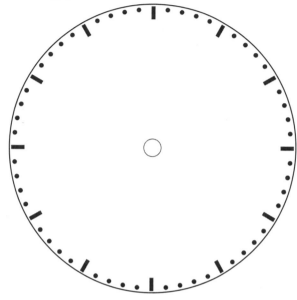

Practice counting the minutes on the clock you assembled yesterday.

Numbers for copywork. Say the numbers as you write them. Find them on your 100's Chart.

70 71 72 73 74

75 76 77 78 79

Using your flashcards, practice your math facts.

Practice counting the minutes on your clock. Narrate to your teacher what you are doing. Remember there are 60 minutes in an hour.

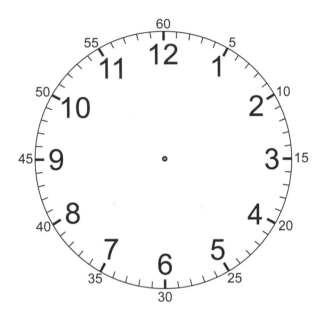

Using your Place Value Village, count out 60 items. Narrate to your teacher what you are doing.

How many 10s? _____   How many 1s ? _____

Numbers to write. Write the numbers from 50–59 from memory. Find them on your 100's chart.

_____

- -

_____

_____

- -

_____

Practice your math facts, using your flashcards. Get ready for a show and tell!

Name_____

Review Time!

Show and tell time! Use this page to show your family or class what you have learned! Count the minutes out loud.

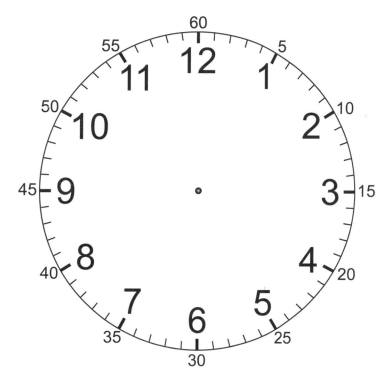

Count by 5s from 0–50. Write the numbers here.

_____

- -

_____
_____

- -

_____

Using 4 colors of construction paper (1 for each shape) cut out 2 circles, 2 squares, 2 rectangles, and 2 triangles. Make a pattern. Narrate what kind of pattern you made. Have fun!

Challenge your family or class to a tally mark scavenger hunt. Help your teacher write tally marks 1–10 on 10 separate index cards. Lay the cards face-up on the table in order. Put out sets of items of your choice (1–10) and set a timer for 3 minutes. See if they can find items to match each card. You be the judge! Did they get the right amount of items for each set of tally marks?

Challenge your family or class to a math fact quiz! Use your flashcards and read the equation out loud but do not tell them the answer! The one who gets the answers the fastest is the winner. Choose a prize for them!

Good job!

Telling Time, Part 2

"Okay, children, dinner is done! Can you two clear away your paper and crayons and help me set the table?" Grandma inquired from the stove. "This stew is just perfect. Charlotte, you set the table, and you go get Grandpa, Charlie. I'll take the bay leaves out of the stew . . . that would be a very unpleasant surprise . . . to come across one of those!" Grandma muttered to herself.

"Yes, Grandma, but will you teach us more about telling time after supper?" Charlotte wanted to know. She placed Grandma's drawing of the clock on the side counter and then carried the plates to the table. "I would be happy to, Charlotte," Grandma smiled at her. "Here are some clean napkins to put in the napkin rings, and I just separated this milk. You may pour it into the pitcher if you think you can do it carefully."

Charlotte nodded and took the stoneware pitcher from the cabinet. She carefully poured the milk into the pitcher, then placed the pitcher on the table. Grandma smiled when Charlotte placed a napkin over the pitcher to keep the flies out.

"Grandpa, Grandma is teaching us how to read the clock!" Charlie exclaimed after the blessing was asked.

"She helped us figure out how many minutes are in an hour. We have to count by 5s just like when we help you pack the boxes of veggies for market."

"That's wonderful, Charlie! Did you two know that I talked to your father today? We decided what day they are going to come and pick you two up. The summer is really winding down, and school is going to start soon for you two," Grandpa's eyes had a mysterious sparkle to them. The children looked at each other.

"Why are your eyes twinkling, Grandpa?" they wanted to know. "Do you know something? Is it exciting? When are Mommy and Daddy coming?" Grandpa chuckled, then he laughed out loud. Grandma looked puzzled too.

Grandpa held up his hands, "One question at a time! First, your parents are going to be here in 10 days. Second, your father told me about a decision he and your mom have made. They are amazed at all you two have learned over the summer, and they want you to continue learning. So . . . they have decided to homeschool you both. Your dad said that they had prayed about it before, but now, they know it's the right thing for you. What do you think about that?"

The children looked at each other, then back at their grandparents. Then they started jumping up and down. "Yippee! We have friends in our church who are homeschooled!" Charlotte exclaimed. "They are always getting to do so many fun things! Last year, when we went to their house, they had a pioneer party. They taught us how to make butter, and we made corncob dolls. It was so fun!"

The children were jumping and dancing around the table by now. "Wait a minute, Charlie!" Charlotte stopped dead in her tracks, "Do you know what this means? This means that we will be right at home when our new baby brother or sister is born! We will get to spend so much time with the baby, and we can help Mommy with it. I wish I knew what 'it' was, then I could stop calling 'it' an 'it'!" Grandpa chuckled.

"Well, come to think of it, Charlotte, we do know what 'it' is! That's another thing your daddy and I talked about today. You two are going to have a new baby sister!" The twins cheered! "Also, we decided that you are going to take Ann and Andy home with you. Your dad is building them a little shed and pen," Grandpa smiled at the looks on his grandchildren's faces.

"Do you two still want to learn more about telling time?" Grandma asked as she poured the leftover stew into an airtight container. "If you do, we better get at it! Your bedtime is in 45 minutes."

In our last lesson, we learned that there are 60 minutes in an hour, and that each number on the clock stands for 5 minutes. Review counting by 5s on your clock.

Get out the clock you assembled and answer these questions about your clock.

How many hands does your clock have? _____

Are they the same length? _____

One hand (the longer one) is the **minute hand**.

The other hand (the shorter one) is the **hour hand**.

The minute hand travels all the way around the clock, and the hour hand travels from one number to the next in one hour. When the hour hand points directly at a number, and the minute hand points directly at the 12, we say it is something o'clock. Example:

3 o'clock
or
3:00

5 o'clock
or
5:00

9 o'clock
or
9:00

Teacher

Time awareness is an abstract concept for most children. Passage of time seems relative to most of us, and children are no different. Explain to your student that even though some days seem to go faster than others, all days are the same length of time. All hours are 60 minutes, and all minutes are the same.

Practice moving the minute and hour hands around the clock as described on the previous page. Let your student become familiar with the clock. Discuss how the hands are different lengths so that we can easily tell whether we are looking at the hour hand or the minute hand. Tell your student that it takes time to learn how to tell time!

Addition practice

4 + 3 = _____   2 + 5 = _____

8 + 1 = _____   5 + 3 = _____

6 + 2 = _____   4 + 4 = _____

Draw a line between the correct time on the clock with the written time on the right.

2 o'clock

8 o'clock

9 o'clock

Use your clock to discuss and review what was learned yesterday. Encourage your student to show you what they remember.

Numbers for copywork. Say them out loud as you write them. Find them on your 100's Chart.

60 61 62 63 64

65 66 67 68 69

Use your flashcards to review math facts. Are you comfortable with all of them? If not, practice those that you have problems remembering.

What time is it? Draw the hands on the clock to show the time. Remember the hour hand should point at the number and the minute hand at the 12. Narrate to your teacher what you are doing.

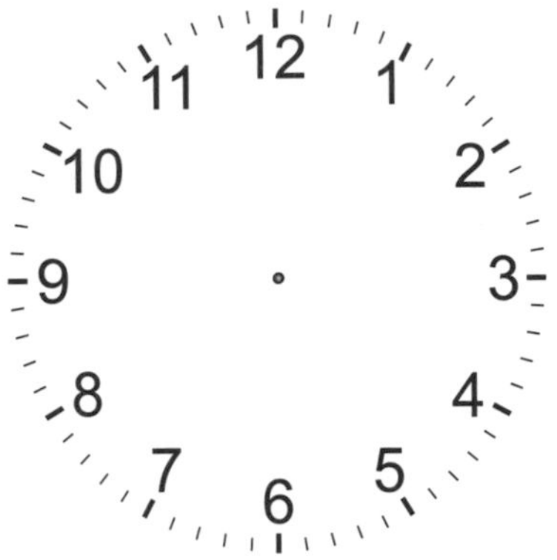

9 o'clock

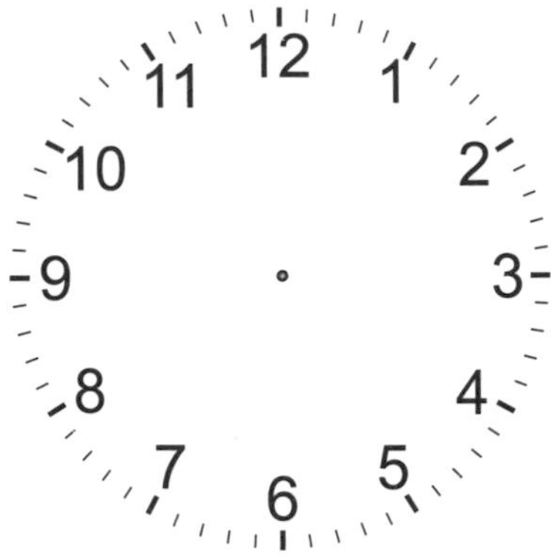

2 o'clock

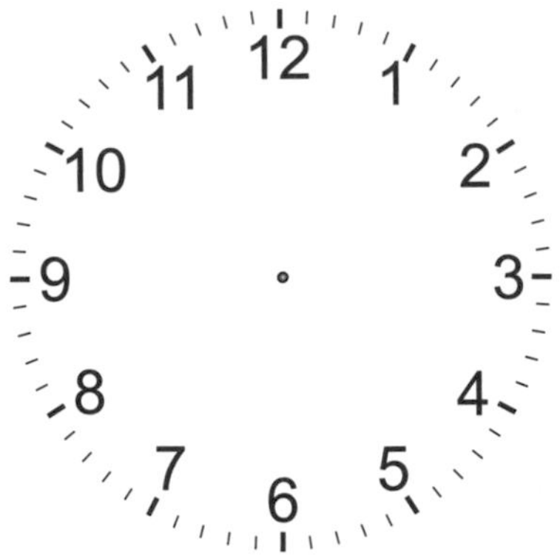

4 o'clock

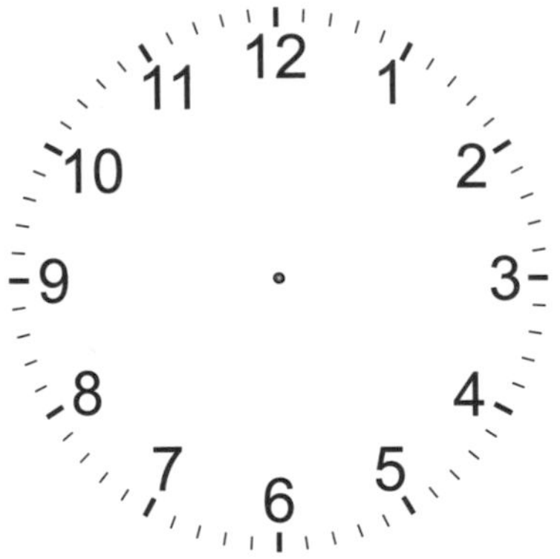

5 o'clock

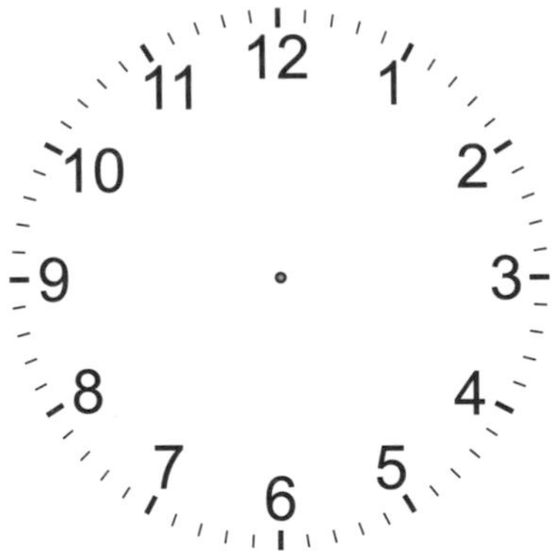

3 o'clock

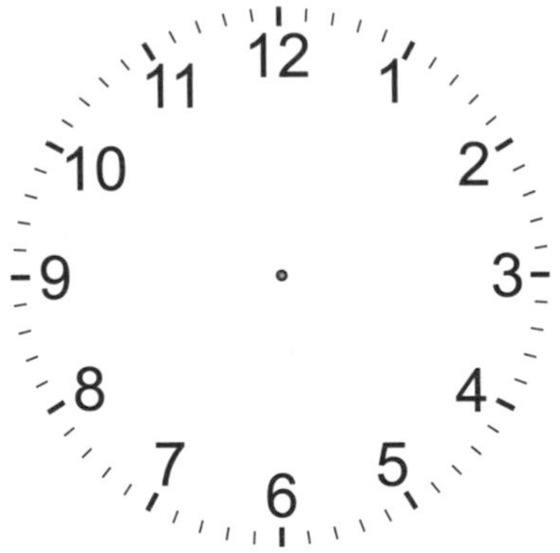

10 o'clock

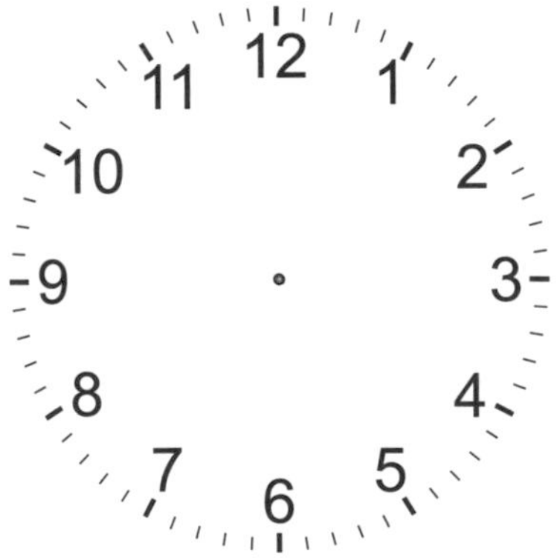

1 o'clock

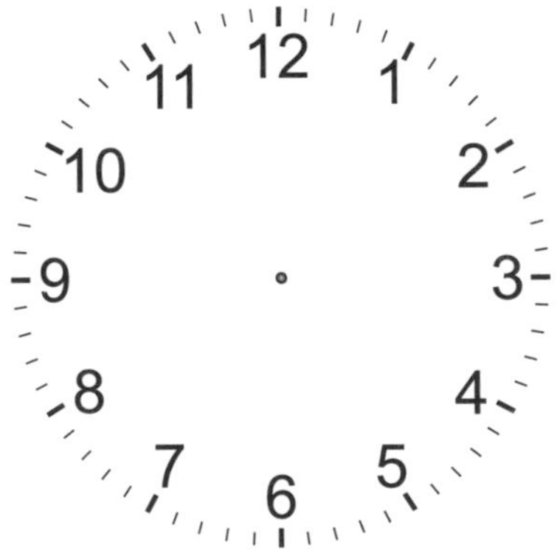

6 o'clock

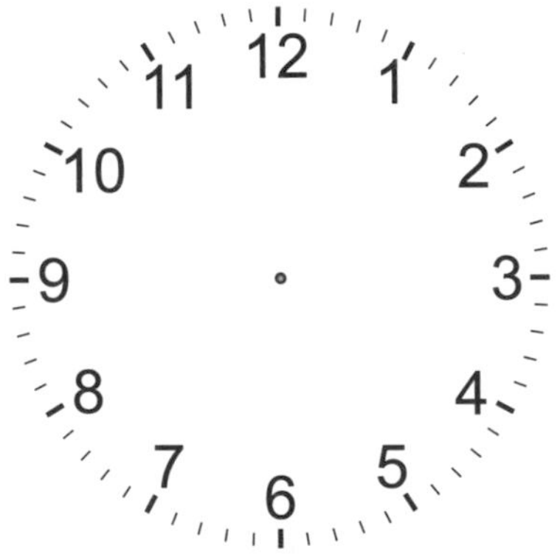

8 o'clock

Numbers for copywork. Say the numbers out loud, and point to them on your clock. Narrate to your teacher about these numbers. What do they show us?

1 2 3 4 5 6

_____

- -

7 8 9 10 11 12

_____

- -

_____

Make two new flashcards with these equations:

$2 + 3 = 5$ and $3 + 5 = 8$

Use your clock to answer.

- Show your teacher the minute hand.

- Now show the hour hand.

- What does the minute hand show, and how do we count the minutes? (by 5s)

- How much does the minute hand move in one hour? (all the way around the clock once)

- How much does the hour hand move every hour? (from one number to the next)

- Show your teacher these times on your clock:

Time	Teacher check
2 o'clock	
8 o'clock	
9 o'clock	
12 o'clock	
6 o'clock	
4 o'clock	

Write the numbers you say when you count by 2s from 0–20.

Use your flashcards to review your math facts.

Review Time!

Today, you are going to use your clock to review and narrate what you have learned about telling time so far. It is important to understand how the clock works before we move on to the next step.

> **Teacher**
>
> *Let your student show you what they have learned with as little coaching as possible. Take note of any concepts that your student doesn't fully understand. Take time to work on those areas before moving onto the next lesson, which includes learning about a.m. and p.m.*

- Use your 100's Chart on the blank side to write the numbers 0–20 by 2s.
- Use your 100's Chart on the blank side to write the numbers 0–50 by 5s.
- Use your 100's Chart on the blank side to write the numbers 0–100 by 10s.

Use your flashcards to review your math facts.

What time is it? Draw the hands on the clock to show the time.

9:00

3:00

6:00

1:00

5:00

Clockwise: hands move in the direction of the clock.

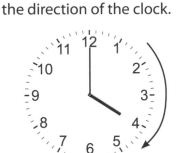

7:00

11:00

Counterclockwise: hands move in the opposite direction of the clock.

Telling Time, Part 3

"Grandma, how many hours are there in a day?" Charlie wanted to know at breakfast the next morning. "Grandpa said that Mom and Dad are coming in 10 days. Sometimes a day seems really long, and sometimes it doesn't. Are different days different lengths?" Charlie smoothed the top of his oatmeal with his spoon. Grandma made the best oatmeal in the world; the twins were sure of it! When they first came to the farm, they said they didn't like oatmeal, but Grandma had told them that they had never tasted hers before. She was right. Brown sugar and bananas . . . yum! (Hey, children hearing this story! Ask your teacher if you can help make oatmeal for tomorrow morning's breakfast, or even today's lunch or supper. The recipe is on the next page!)

Grandma smiled over her glasses at Charlie. She was working on a cross-stitch blanket for the new baby. "There are 24 hours in every single day, Charlie. They are all the same length. Sometimes when we are super busy, like we have been with the harvest, time seems to go faster." Charlie stared at the clock.

"But, Grandma, the numbers on the clock only go to 12. Why?"

"Because the hour hand goes around the clock two whole times in one day. Twelve plus 12 is 24. Come here, Charlie and Charlotte, I will show you what I mean. When the hands go around the first time, we call that a.m. This is the morning. The second time they go around is the afternoon and evening."

"So," continued Grandma, "There are two 12 o'clocks, two 1 o'clocks, two 2 o'clocks, and so on and so forth. Do you two understand?" The children looked at each other with raised eyebrows. "Umm . . . Grandma, I think we better practice for a while. I'm sure we will understand better if we do," Charlie said. Grandma and Charlotte nodded in agreement. You practice too. It's important to practice a new concept until you know it well.

Teacher

You may or may not want to explain to your student that the before noon acronym, a.m., stands for ante meridian, and the afternoon acronym, p.m., stands for post meridian, Latin words which mean "before noon" and "after noon." You decide whether or not this would confuse your student. You may choose to simply say, "When you are a bit older, I will explain what a.m. and p.m. stand for."

Grandma's "scruptdelicious" oatmeal. Makes 6-8 (large) servings

4 1/2 cups of water

1 tsp of salt

1 tsp pure vanilla extract

1/2 tbs of cinnamon

1/4 tsp nutmeg

3 cups of whole rolled oats

(optional, but so yummy!) 1/4 raisins

Stir everything together in medium sized pot and bring to a boil over a medium heat.

Once at a boil, turn down to low, and let simmer until oats are tender. Stir occasionally.

Serve with sliced banana and a sprinkling of light brown sugar, or, if you prefer, honey.

Yummmm! Warm and sweet!

Make flashcards to help you learn about telling time. Use large index cards, bright colors, and, if you have them, stickers, to make your cards. Write one concept on each card. Write the answer on the back. Every day during this lesson, start by doing these clock exercises. You may use your clock to demonstrate.

For Flashcards

- How many minutes are in an hour?

- How many hours are in a day?

- How many times does the hour hand go all the way around the clock in one day?

- What does the minute hand do every hour?

- What does the hour hand do every hour?

- When the hour hand is pointing directly at a number, and the minute hand is pointing directly at the 12, we say it is _____?

- Make a flashcard showing what you do in the a.m. hours. Make another one showing what you do in the p.m. hours. Good job!

After your flashcards are completed, punch a hole in the top left corner of each card and place them on a ring. Store them in your container with your other flashcards and manipulatives.

Review time concepts with your flashcards.

Draw numbers and hands on the clocks to match the times. Draw a picture in the box under each picture showing something you might do at that time.

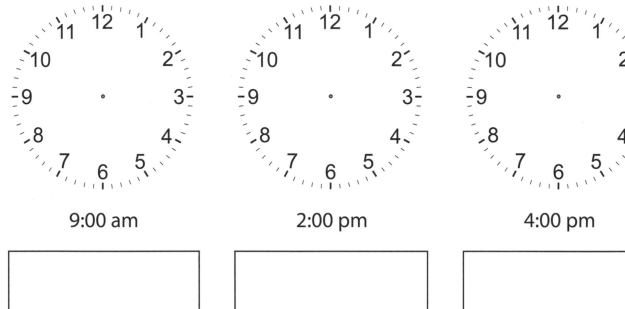

9:00 am   2:00 pm   4:00 pm

Count by 5s, 5–50. Write the numbers in the squares.

Match the clocks with the correct time.

11 o'clock

4 o'clock

9 o'clock

2 o'clock

12 o'clock

Practice time concepts with your flashcards.

Numbers for copywork. Say the words out loud as you write them. Find them on your 100's Chart.

80 81 82 83 84

---

85 86 87 88 89

Count by 10s, 10–100. Write the numbers in the squares.

Review time concepts with your flashcards. Use your clock to show your teacher these times. Draw the time on the clocks. Draw a line to match the time to the correct clock.

6 o'clock

3 o'clock

12 o'clock

10 o'clock

5 o'clock

1 o'clock

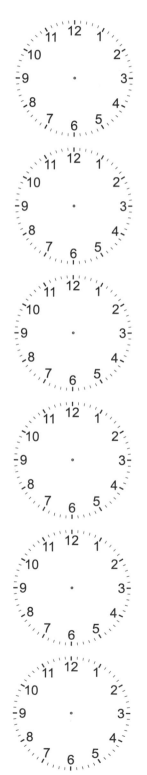

Addition practice

3 + 7 = _____   2 + 4 = _____

9 + 1 = _____   5 + 5 = _____

7 + 2 = _____   4 + 3 = _____

Numbers for copywork. Say the numbers as you write them. Find them on your 100's Chart.

70 71 72 73 74

75 76 77 78 79

Review time!

Today, you are going to make a poster.

You will need:

- ☐ A piece of poster board (alternatives: 6 pieces of construction paper or other sturdy paper, taped together to make a large piece of paper)
- ☐ A drinking glass to use as a circle stencil
- ☐ Crayons, markers, or colored pencils
- ☐ Stickers (optional)
- ☐ Your clock concepts flashcards

Directions:

1. Ask your teacher to help you trace 24 circles on your paper. You will want to trace 12 circles on one side of the poster and 12 on the other. Leave enough room next to each circle to draw a small picture.

2. On one side, draw a sun and write "a.m., Before Noon." On the other side, draw a moon and write "p.m. After Noon."

3. Now make each circle into a clock and fill in the times 1 o'clock through 12 o'clock. Draw a small picture showing what you do at that time every day.

4. Discuss the fact that you are still sleeping when it turns to the a.m. hours.

5. Have a show and tell for your family or class using your poster.

Connect the dots 1 to 40 and then color the image!

Introducing Simple Fractions, Part 1

"Grandma, I think Charlie's piece of pie is bigger than mine," Charlotte held up her plate to inspect her dessert more closely. "Yes, I'm sure it is! Look!" Grandma came over, took both plates and held them up to look at them.

"You're right, Charlotte. I thought I cut the pie into equal pieces, but I must have been off just a little. Here, you may have a bit more." Grandma brought the pie to the table and sliced a little more off for Charlotte.

"How do you cut a pie so that every piece is the same, Grandma?" Charlie asked around his fork. "Oops, sorry, Grandma," he said after swallowing his food. Grandma was always telling him to not talk while he was chewing food. Grandma smiled at him. She was proud that he had caught himself. "Well, Charlie, it's called fractions.

"First you cut the pie. This is called a half, which is also written like this:

$$\frac{1}{2}$$

"Here, Children, you can practice drawing fractions on this piece of paper. It really is quite fun!"

Grandma smiled as she watched the children draw circles on their papers and then carefully make fractions. "Remember, Children, when you have a fraction, that means all of the parts are equal. Do you remember what equal means?"

The children nodded. "Yes, Grandma, that means two things are exactly the same," Charlotte answered. "Is this equal, Grandma?" Charlie held up his paper for his grandma to inspect. It was a lot harder than it looked to make his fraction exactly equal!

"Yes, I believe it is, Charlie. You two finish up your pie now, and go brush your teeth and take your baths. It's almost your bedtime!" Grandma said as she glanced at the kitchen clock.

Color the true fractions red. Remember, a true fraction is one that each "piece" is exactly the same. Cross out the ones that are not true fractions.

Now it's your turn. Draw a line to "cut" each of the shapes exactly in half.

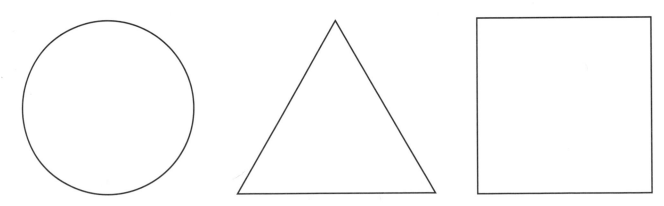

Using your time concepts flashcards, review what you have learned about telling time.

Match the times with the correct clock.

9 o'clock

11 o'clock

7 o'clock

12 o'clock

Addition practice

3 + 6 = _____   4 + 4 = _____   7 + 2 = _____

5 + 3 = _____   5 + 5 = _____   3 + 3 = _____

Color each true fraction blue.

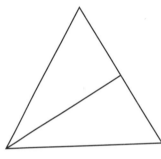 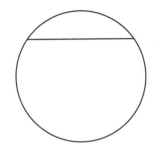 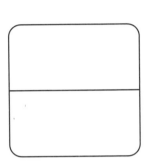

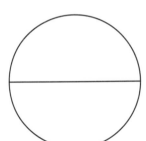 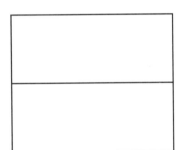 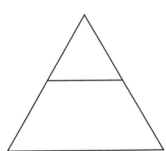

Use your time concepts flashcards to review these questions. Write the answers here.

How many hours are in one day? _____

How many minutes are in one hour? _____

How many times does the hour hand go all the way around the clock in one day?

_____

How do the minute and hour hands work together? (Explain to your teacher.)

What is the highest number on the clock? _____

"Cut" each of these shapes in half by drawing a line on the shapes.

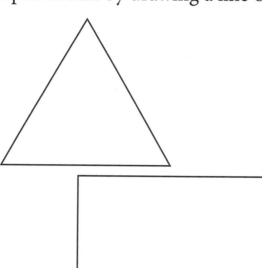
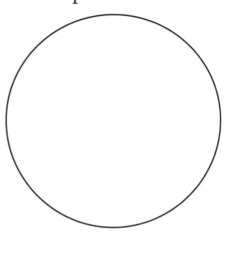

Use your clock to show your teacher these times.

11 o'clock	3 o'clock	9 o'clock
1 o'clock	6 o'clock	12 o'clock

Counting by 2s. Fill in the squares with the numbers you say when you count by 2s, 2–20.

Use your Place Value Village to count out 48 items.

How many groups of 10? _____

How many groups of 1? _____

Numbers to write. From memory, write the numbers 0–17.

_____

- -

_____
_____

- -

_____
_____

- -

_____

Color each true fraction yellow.

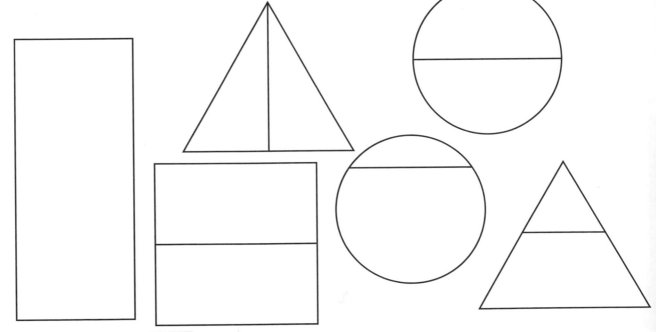

Review Time!

Help the twins write a letter to their parents. Show them what we have learned this week.

Dear Mom and Dad,

This week, we have been learning about fractions. Grandma told us that all true fractions have equal parts. These are true fractions. ("Cut" these shapes into equal halves.)

 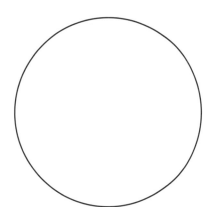 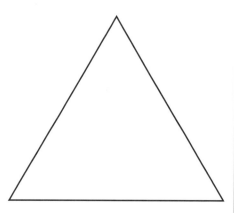

We are really good at writing numbers too. (Write the numbers 20–29 from memory)

_____

_____

_____

_____

We have also been learning a lot about telling time! (Match the time to the correct clock.)

5 o'clock

3 o'clock

11 o'clock

6 o'clock

2 o'clock

1 o'clock

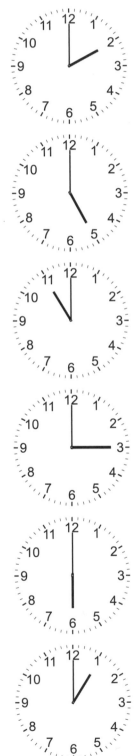

Love, Charlotte, Charlie, and our friend, _____

To the twins, it seemed that time was going by faster and faster. Their visit was almost over, and soon they would be going home. Just that morning, they had talked to their parents on the phone. Mommy had sounded so excited, and Daddy had told them that the sheep pen was almost finished. Since they had found out that they were going to be homeschooled, the twins were even more excited about going home. They had talked at night when the lights were off, and they had made quite a list of projects they wanted to do with Mommy and Daddy!

After supper, the children and their grandparents gathered in the family room. Grandpa was teaching the children how to play checkers. It was very cozy with the fire crackling away in the fireplace. The twins were going to miss these fun evenings with Grandma and Grandpa.

"You know, children, once you understand what a half is, you can learn about all kinds of fractions," Grandma said. She was working on a pretty cross-stitch for the new baby. The children were kneeling next to the coffee table drawing pictures. "Look, do you see how I have this cross-stitch design sectioned off? This is a large and complicated design, so I have it divided evenly to make sure I don't make a mistake in the colors I'm using. Come see." The children got up to inspect Grandma's needlework.

"You have it divided into four sections. What fraction is that, Grandma?" Charlotte asked.

"That is called a fourth," Grandma answered as she snipped a thread with a pair of tiny scissors. "You can draw a fourth from a half. You have to draw it like this; first you draw a half, then you cut each half in half. This is called a fourth because there are 4 equal pieces. No matter what your fraction is, all the pieces have to be the same size. Otherwise it's not a true fraction."

A fourth is also written

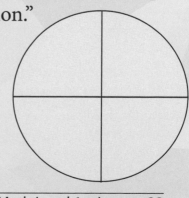

Color the true fractions blue.

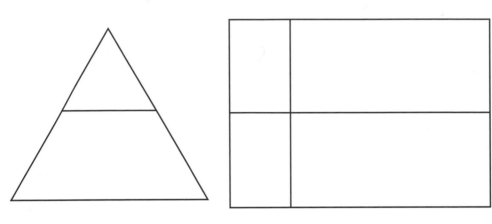

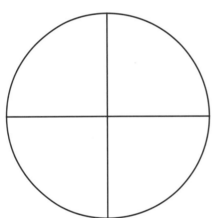  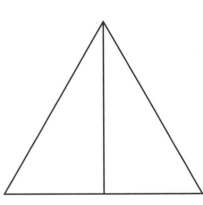

Numbers to write. Write the numbers you say when you count by 5s from 0–50. Try not to look at your 100's Chart.

_____

- -

_____

- -

_____

Write the correct time under each clock. Read the time of each clock to your teacher. The first one is done for you. When we see 2:00, we read it as "two o'clock."

4:00

_____

_____

_____

_____

_____

_____

Addition practice

4 + 3 = _____   2 + 5 = _____

8 + 1 = _____   5 + 3 = _____

6 + 2 = _____   4 + 4 = _____

Use your time concept cards to review.

Use your clock to show your teacher these times.

11 o'clock   4 o'clock

9 o'clock   2 o'clock

5 o'clock   7 o'clock

As you count by 2s from 0–20.

_____

- -

_____
_____

- -

As you count by 5s from 0–50.

_____

- -

_____
_____

- -

Write the fraction under each one. The first one is done for you.

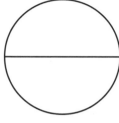  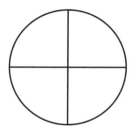

1
___
2 ___   ___   ___
___   ___   ___

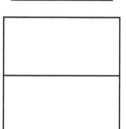 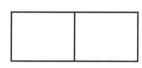

___   ___   ___
___   ___   ___

Numbers to write. From memory, write the numbers from 30–39.

_____

- - - - - - - - - - - - - - - - - - -

_____

_____

- - - - - - - - - - - - - - - - - - -

_____

Match the clocks with the correct time.

1 o'clock

7 o'clock

11 o'clock

4 o'clock

2 o'clock

12 o'clock

9 o'clock

Use your time concepts flashcards to review what you have learned about the clock and telling time. Use your clock to answer these questions. Narrate the answers to your teacher.

1. Which is the minute hand?

2. Which is the hour hand?

3. What does the minute hand do in one hour?

4. What does the hour hand do in one hour?

5. How many times does the hour hand go all the way around the clock in one day?

6. In which direction do the hands on the clock turn?

7. Tell anything else you know about telling time.

Use your Place Value Village to count out these numbers of items. Answer the questions.

1. Count 59 items. How many groups of 10? _____

    How many groups of 1? _____   Write the number here: _____

2. Count out 22 items. How many groups of 10? _____

    How many groups of 1? _____   Write the number here: _____

3. Count out 17 items. How many groups of 10? _____

    How many groups of 1? _____   Write the number here: _____

On the blank side of your 100's Chart, write in the numbers as you say them.

   Count by 2s from 0–20.

   Count by 5s from 0–50.

   Count by 10s from 0–100.

Review Time! "Cut" or divide each of these shapes into fractions. You choose if you want fourths or halves. Color the halves blue and the fourths red.

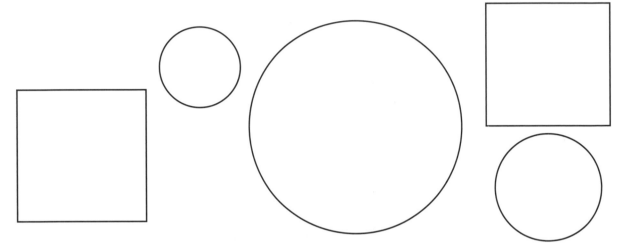

Numbers to write. Write the numbers from 60–69, find them on your 100's Chart.

_____

- -

_____
_____

- -

_____

Write the numbers from 70–79, then find them on your 100's Chart.

_____

- -

_____
_____

- -

_____

Use your math facts flashcards to review your facts.

Introduction to Subtraction

"Grandpa, is there anything else you want to teach us about numbers before we go home tomorrow?" Charlie asked hopefully. The children and their grandparents were eating a delicious breakfast of scrambled eggs and Grandma's famous cinnamon buns. It was going to be a very busy day getting ready to go home. Grandma had already started their laundry, and the twins had the chore of emptying out the dresser and closet they had been using all summer.

MENU
Grandma's
Cinnamon
Buns

"You really love numbers, don't you, Charlie?" Grandpa's eyes twinkled as he smiled at his grandson. "Well, there is one thing I haven't taught you . . . and it's something that I love doing with Grandma's cinnamon buns!" The twins looked at each other with raised eyebrows. What in the world was he talking about? What did Grandma's cinnamon buns have to do with learning math concepts?

"Do you give up?" Grandpa chuckled. They nodded their heads. "Well, when Grandma takes her cinnamon buns out of the oven, and puts them on the table, there are 10 in the pan. Right? Then I reach over and take 2! Now how many are left?" The twins got up on their knees to look into the pan. Charlotte pointed as she counted.

"There would be 8 left, Grandpa. But what does that have to do with math and learning something new with numbers?" the twins still looked puzzled. Maybe Grandpa was pulling their leg again. He was good at that! Grandpa chuckled again.

"Well, children, you have already learned how to do addition, right?" They nodded. "What I just showed you is the opposite of addition. Think about it. When you add, you take two or more sets of things and add them together to make a bigger number. What I just did with Grandma's cinnamon buns was called subtraction. Subtraction is the opposite of addition, because it makes something smaller. Grandma makes a pan of 10 buns. I ate 2 of them. There are 8 buns left!"

"Oh, we understand! That's really fun, Grandpa! Let us try it." The twins ran to get a piece of paper and a pencil. "Here, Grandpa, show us how to write it, please." Grandpa took the paper and wrote:

"This is a subtraction sign. When we write a subtraction equation, we write it like this:

$$10 - 2 = 8$$

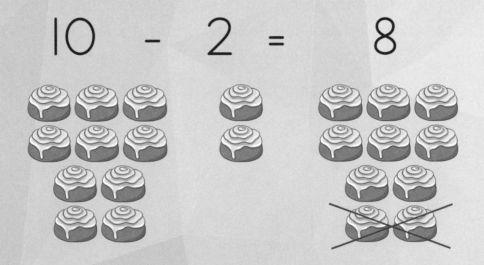

Now you try it! Trace the subtraction sign.

Remember, when you see this sign in an equation, it means you are making something smaller. Try it! The first one is done for you.

3 − 2 = 1

4 − 3 = ____

6 − 2 = ____

5 − 2 = ____

7 − 3 = ____

2 − 1 = ____

Make each shape into the correct fraction.

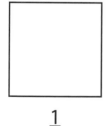
$\frac{1}{2}$

$\frac{1}{4}$

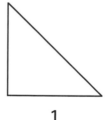
$\frac{1}{2}$

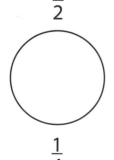
$\frac{1}{4}$

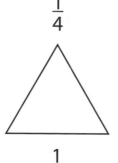
$\frac{1}{2}$

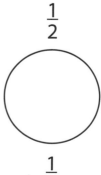
$\frac{1}{4}$

Solve these subtraction equations. Use your small counting items. The first one is done for you.

4 – 2 = 2

6 – 4 = _____

5 – 3 = _____

3 – 1 = _____

7 – 2 = _____

9 – 4 = _____

Numbers for copywork. Say the numbers as you write them. Find them on your 100's chart.

90   91   92   93   94

---

95   96   97   98   99

Match the clocks with the correct time.

5 o'clock

2 o'clock

1 o'clock

8 o'clock

12 o'clock

4 o'clock

9 o'clock

Use your small counting items to solve these subtraction equations. Narrate to your teacher what you are doing.

2 – 1 = _____   7 – 3 = _____

3 – 2 = _____   8 – 2 = _____

5 – 4 = _____   5 – 1 = _____

Explain to your teacher how subtraction is the opposite of addition. (Use your counting items to show this.)

Use your small counting items to solve these equations. Narrate to your teacher what you are doing.

$4 - 1 =$ _____ $7 - 2 =$ _____

$5 - 2 =$ _____ $2 - 1 =$ _____

$6 - 4 =$ _____ $9 - 8 =$ _____

In the space below, draw and color a pattern using all the shapes you have learned. Explain your pattern to your teacher.

 My shape pattern:

Review Time!

Today, you are going to make a poster or a book about what you have learned about subtraction. Use pictures from an old magazine, stickers, or pictures you draw. Make it as nice as you can! Narrate to your teacher what you have learned.

Numbers for copywork. Say the numbers as you write them. Find them on your 100's Chart.

80 81 82 83 84

85 86 87 88 89

Subtraction - 1

The children thought subtraction was a lot of fun. Grandpa hadn't been pulling their leg after all! The next morning while the twins were upstairs in the bedroom, cleaning out their closet and dresser, they talked about the new number concept. They were going home with Mom and Dad today. Grandma said that they would be here in three hours. That meant when this hour was done they would have 2 hours. They now knew that this was subtraction.

"Charlie, if you think about it, subtraction is like counting backwards!" Charlotte exclaimed. "If you start at 10 and take away 1, you have 9. If you take 1 away from 9, you have 8. If you take 1 away from 8, you have 7. See what I mean?" Charlie nodded his head. "Let's count our shirts before we pack them, and then subtract or take away 1 every time we pack 1 in the suitcase," Charlotte suggested.

$$8 - 1 = 7 \qquad 7 - 1 = 6 \qquad 6 - 1 = 5 \qquad 5 - 1 = 4 \qquad 4 - 1 = 3$$

"Ok! We have 8 shirts. . . . Let's see, if we pack 1, that is 7 shirts. If we pack another 1, that is 6 shirts, then 5, then 4, then 3, then 2, then 1! That's all of them," Charlie counted out loud as they folded and stacked their shirts neatly in the corner of their large suitcase.

Next, they counted their socks. This was easy to do, because Grandma had shown them how to ball their socks up into pairs. They each counted 7 pairs of socks. Charlotte counted backward as she packed her socks into the other corner of the suitcase. "7, 6, 5, 4, 3, 2, 1, . . . 1!" she said.

"Children!" It was Grandma calling them from the bottom of the stairs. "Children, your parents are here!"

Charlotte and Charlie looked at each other and squealed. Together they zipped up the suitcase, now full of their clothes, and skipped down the stairs.

Everyone was talking at once! Mom and Dad had to kiss each of the children at least 5 times, and Grandma ran around gathering the last of the children's belongings; artwork, craft projects and rubber boots were all piled into a cardboard box. Grandpa, Dad, and Charlie went out to load the lambs into the trailer, while Grandma and Mom packed lunches for the trip home.

Charlotte kept touching Mom's tummy. She had never seen her mommy look so beautiful, and her tummy was now a round bump where Charlotte's baby sister was growing, all safe and warm. Charlotte loved to think about that little baby girl inside her mommy. Grandma had explained to her that her little sister was all curled up, warm and protected, while she developed strong lungs and a strong heart to live on the outside of Mommy. It made her so happy to know that she would soon be able to hold her! Mom caught Charlotte's eye and smiled at her. She knew what Charlotte was thinking.

"Mommy and Grandma, I know what my favorite pattern in the world is," Charlotte told them, as she stood between them. She had been thinking about this since she had found out about the baby; their baby.

"What's that, Charlotte," Mommy said, smiling down at Charlotte's happy face. Mom couldn't believe how much Charlotte had grown over the summer, and there was a new gap where a tooth used to be.

Charlotte laid her hand on Mommy's tummy and was rewarded with a kick from the baby inside. Charlotte's smile got even bigger, and she said, "The pattern of babies! I love how God made it that babies grow inside of mommies, all safe and warm, until they are big enough to be outside in the world. Yup! Babies are definitely my favorite pattern!"

The men and Charlie came into the kitchen then. It was time to say "goodbye." There were hugs and kisses and even a few tears. It had been a wonderful summer, and the promise of an exciting fall and winter lay before them.

Explore subtraction using small counting items. Count out 10 items. Take 1 away. How many are left? Take another 1 away. Now how many are left? Keep doing this until you do not have any left. Do this several times, until you are comfortable with the concept.

10 – 1 = _____   5 – 1 = _____

9 – 1 = _____   4 – 1 = _____

8 – 1 = _____   3 – 1 = _____

7 – 1 = _____   2 – 1 = _____

6 – 1 = _____   1 – 1 = _____

Fraction practice. Color all the halves blue and all the quarters yellow.

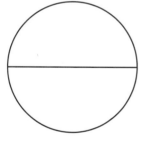
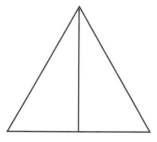
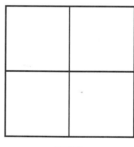
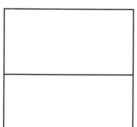
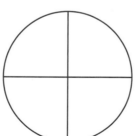
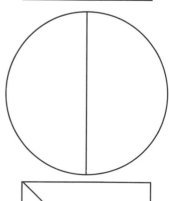
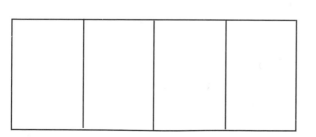

Subtraction practice. Use your counting items to solve these equations.

$4 - 1 =$ _____ $4 - 3 =$ _____

$6 - 2 =$ _____ $8 - 4 =$ _____

$9 - 4 =$ _____ $10 - 1 =$ _____

Addition is the opposite of subtraction. Solve these addition equations and compare them to the equations above. Do you see a pattern? Talk to your teacher about what you see.

$3 + 1 =$ _____ $1 + 3 =$ _____

$4 + 2 =$ _____ $4 + 4 =$ _____

$5 + 4 =$ _____ $9 + 1 =$ _____

Write the correct time under the clocks. Read the time of each clock to your teacher. The first one is done for you.

1:00

_____

_____

_____

_____

_____

Color all the true fractions green.

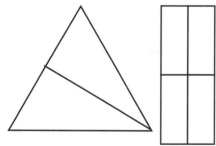
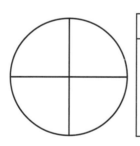

Numbers to write. Write the numbers between 40–49. Say them as you write them and then find them on your 100's Chart.

Trace the numbers counting backward. Say them as you trace them.

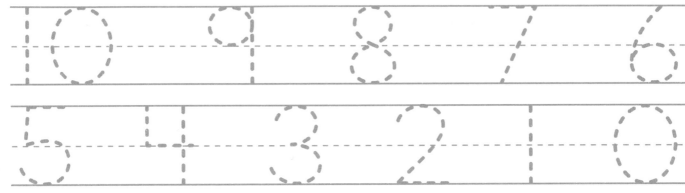

Solve these subtraction problems.

9 – 1 = _____   9 – 3 = _____

4 – 2 = _____   8 – 5 = _____

5 – 3 = _____   5 – 4 = _____

Fill in the hours on this clock's face. Make it say 10 o'clock.

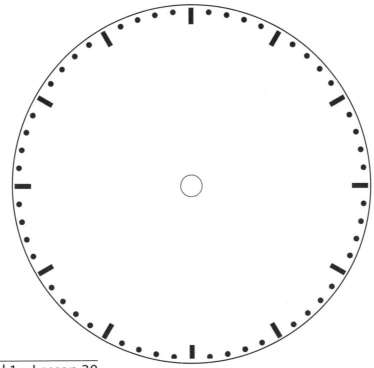

Review Time!

Write the numbers from 1–9 backward. Say them out loud as you write them.

_____

- -

_____

Make a pattern using the shapes you have learned. Explain the pattern to your teacher.

 My pattern:

Review your math fact flashcards.

Review your time/clock concepts flashcards.

On your 100's Chart (on the blank side), fill in the numbers you say when you skip count by 2s, from 0–20. Now fill in the numbers you say when you skip count by 5s, from 0–50. Fill in the numbers you say when you skip count by 10s, from 0–100.

Count how many are in each group of objects or people. Put the number of the first group in the first circle under it. Put the number of the second group in the next circle. Then solve the problem and put the answer in the last circle.

$$\bigcirc ? \ - \ \bigcirc ? \ = \ \bigcirc ?$$

$$\bigcirc ? \ - \ \bigcirc ? \ = \ \bigcirc ?$$

$$\bigcirc ? \ - \ \bigcirc ? \ = \ \bigcirc ?$$

0 1 2 3 4 5 6 7 8 9 + −
10 11 12 13 14 15 16 17 18 19 20 =

Review of Shapes

This week we are going to review shapes. Each day, there will be an activity to enforce and review one shape. The week will end with a review of all the shapes together.

Square

A square has four equal sides. It has four corners that are right angles.

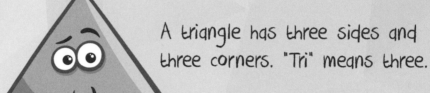

A triangle has three sides and three corners. "Tri" means three.

Triangle

A circle is a shape with no corners.

Circle

A rectangle is a shape with four corners at right angles. It has four sides – two are long and two are shorter.

Rectangle

Circles

Trace and then write the word "circle" below. Trace the circle.

Color all of the circles green.

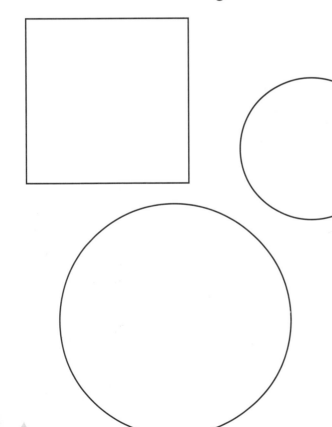

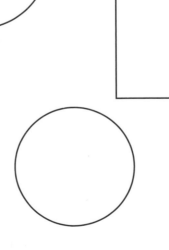

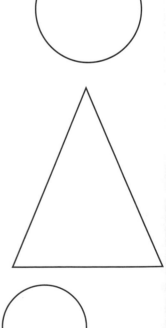

In the space below, either draw a picture using only circles, or go on a "circle hunt" and draw what you find.

My circles:

Squares

Trace and then write the word "square" below. Trace the square.

Color all of the squares blue.

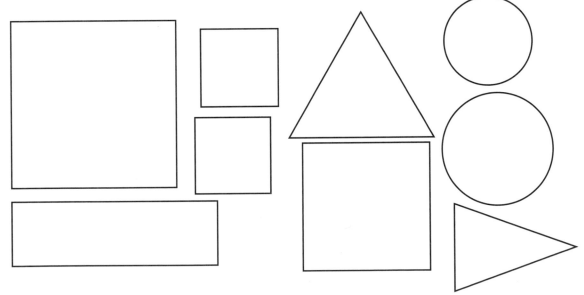

How many sides does a square have? _____

Are they all the same length? yes or no _____

How many corners does a square have? _____

Trace the words.

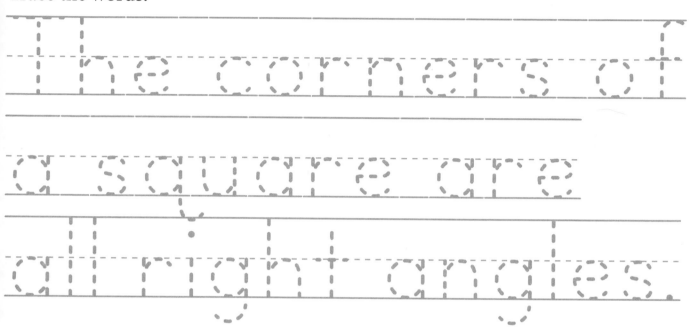

The corners of
a square are
all right angles.

In the space below, either draw a picture using only squares, or go on a "square hunt" and draw what you find.

 My squares:

Rectangle

Trace and then write the word "rectangle" below. Trace the rectangle.

rectangle

Color all of the rectangles blue.

How many sides does a rectangle have? _____

Are they all the same length? yes or no _____

How many corners does a rectangle have? _____

Trace the words.

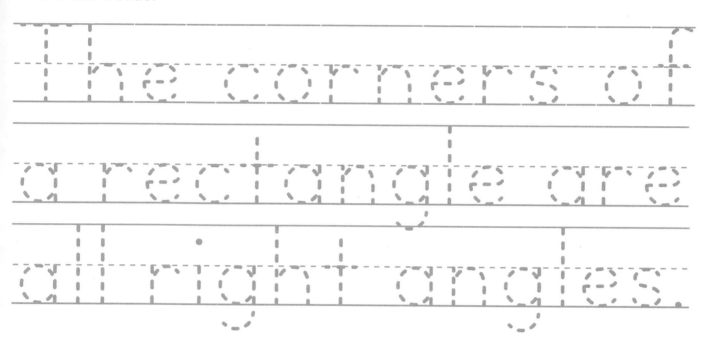

The corners of
a rectangle are
all right angles.

In the space below, either draw a picture using only rectangles, or go on a "rectangle hunt" and draw what you find.

 My rectangles:

Triangles

Trace and then write the word "triangle" below. Trace the triangles.

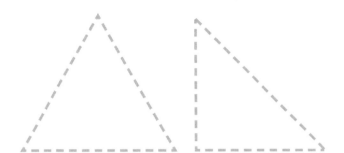

Color all of the triangles yellow. All triangles have 3 sides and 3 corners.

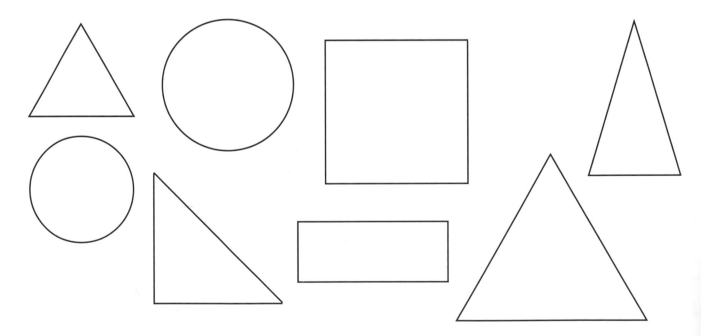

How many sides does a triangle have? _____

How many corners does a triangle have? _____

In the space below, either draw a picture using only triangles, or go on a "triangle hunt" and draw what you find.

My triangles:

Review Time!

Color all the circles green, all the squares blue, all the rectangles red, and all the triangles yellow.

Which shapes have 4 sides and 4 corners? _____

_____

Which shape has no corners at all? _____

Which shape has 3 sides and 3 corners? _____

Which shape has 2 long sides and 2 shorter sides? _____

This week we are going to review place value up to 100. You will need your Place Value Village, Place Value Village Counting Mat, and counting items. Each day you will be counting out a number of items and writing the numbers on your mat. Each day, you will be continuing from the point where you left off the day before. Do not erase your numbers until the end of the week.

The HUNDREDS' house

Remember: Only 9 groups of a hundred may live here!

Today we are going to count from 0–25. Use your Place Value Village, Place Value Village Counting Mat, and small counting items. As you count, write the numbers on the mat. Narrate to your teacher what you are doing.

Answer these questions about these numbers.

19   How many 10s? _____   How many 1s? _____

10   How many 10s? _____   How many 1s? _____

23   How many 10s? _____   How many 1s? _____

29   How many 10s? _____   How many 1s? _____

18   How many 10s? _____   How many 1s? _____

Numbers for copywork. Say them as you write them. Find them on your 100's Chart.

20 21 22 23 24

25 26 27 28 29

Today we are going to count from 26–50. Use your Place Value Village, Place Value Village Counting Mat, and small counting items. As you count, write the numbers on the mat. Narrate to your teacher what you are doing.

Answer these questions about these numbers.

47   How many 10s? _____   How many 1s? _____

39   How many 10s? _____   How many 1s? _____

50   How many 10s? _____   How many 1s? _____

29   How many 10s? _____   How many 1s? _____

33   How many 10s? _____   How many 1s? _____

Numbers for copywork. Say them as you write them. Find them on your 100's Chart.

30 31 32 33 34

35 36 37 38 39

Today we are going to count from 51–75. Use your Place Value Village, Place Value Village Counting Mat, and small counting items. As you count, write the numbers on the mat. Narrate to your teacher what you are doing.

Answer the questions about the numbers.

59   How many 10s? _____   How many 1s? _____

70   How many 10s? _____   How many 1s? _____

63   How many 10s? _____   How many 1s? _____

52   How many 10s? _____   How many 1s? _____

67   How many 10s? _____   How many 1s? _____

Numbers for copywork. Say them as you write them. Find them on your 100's Chart.

50 51 52 53 54

55 56 57 58 59

Today we are going to count from 76–100. Use your Place Value Village, Place Value Village Counting Mat, and small counting items. As you count, write the numbers on the mat. Narrate to your teacher what you are doing.

Answer these questions about these numbers.

79   How many 10s? _____   How many 1s? _____

82   How many 10s? _____   How many 1s? _____

99   How many 10s? _____   How many 1s? _____

89   How many 10s? _____   How many 1s? _____

92   How many 10s? _____   How many 1s? _____

Numbers for copywork. Say them as you write them. Find them on your 100's Chart.

80 81 82 83 84

85 86 87 88 89

Review Time!

We have reached 100! Good job.

Today we are going to write all the numbers, from 0 to 100. Using the blank side of your 100's Chart, write all the numbers.

Try not to look at the filled-in side. Say the numbers out loud as you write them. How did you do? Did you remember them all? Yes _____ No _____

Review of Addition

This week we are going to review the concept of addition and the math facts you have learned while doing this book. You will need your Addition Mat (horizontal), number cards 0–10, small counting items, and the flashcards you have created.

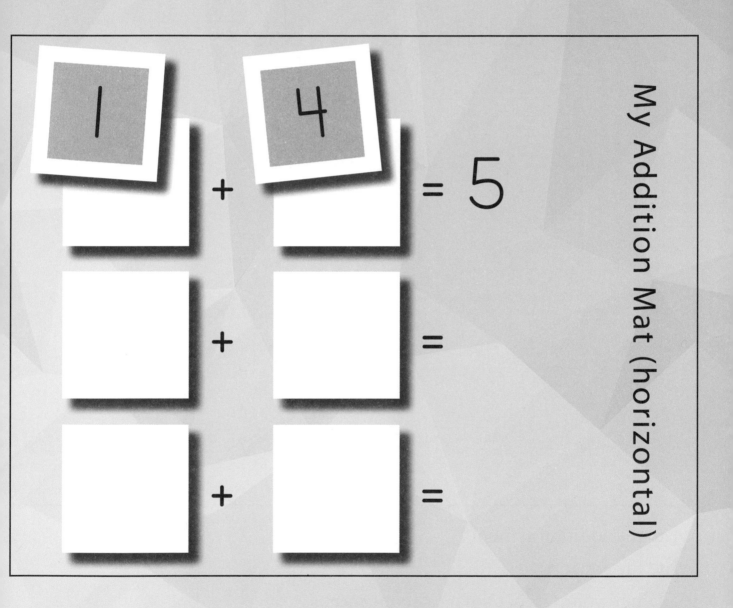

My Addition Mat (horizontal)

$1 + 4 = 5$

Using your Addition Mat (horizontal), number cards 0–10, and small counting items, make 8 addition equations. Narrate to your teacher what you are doing. Write your equations in the space below.

 My addition equations:

Write the addition symbol. _____

Write the equal sign. _____

Explain to your teacher what each one means.

Use your flashcards to review your math facts.

Match the sets with the equations and write the answers.

4 + 2 = _____

3 + 1 = _____

1 + 2 = _____

3 + 4 = _____

4 + 1 = _____

Today, we are going to practice adding vertically. Use your Addition Mat (vertical), number cards 0–10, and small counting items.

Make 8 addition equations. Narrate to your teacher what you are doing. Write your equations in the space.

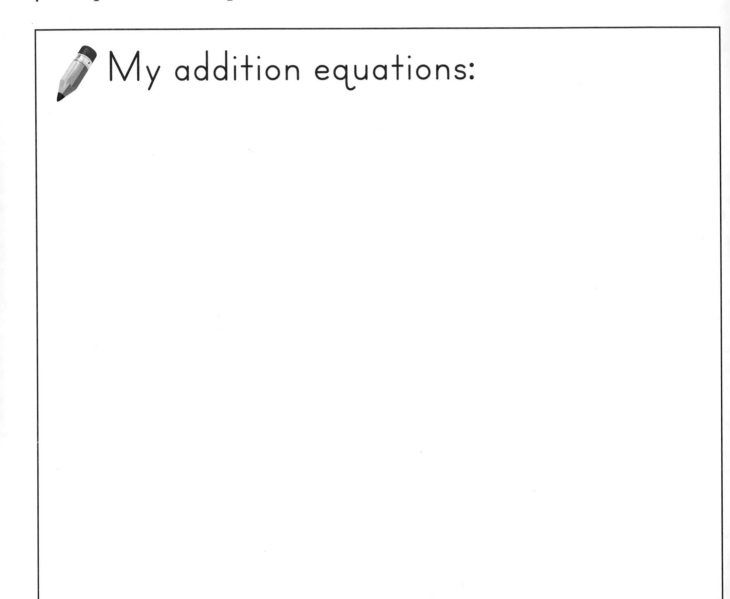

✏️ My addition equations:

Make some addition equations for your teacher to solve! Then use your flashcards to review your math facts.

Place all of your 0–10 number cards face up in a row.

Write 10 addition equations without the answer on small pieces of paper. Turn them all face down on the table. As you turn them over, solve the equations and place them under the number that shows the answer.

Make a hop-scotch pattern and write addition equations in them. When you land on an equation, answer it! Challenge your teacher to a game of "equation hop-scotch!"

Review Time!

Today, you are going to make an addition poster! Cut out pictures from old magazines. (The pictures can be of animals, plants, children, cars, food items, or anything you wish, as long as they are small — no larger than 4 inches across.)

Make sets for addition equations with your pictures. Write nice and big! Make a nice poster to show your family, or maybe you can hang it in your bedroom. Narrate to your teacher everything you have learned about addition.

When we count 1, 2, 3, 4, 5, . . . we are counting by 1s. We can also count by 2s, 5s, 10s, and any other number we want. This is called skip counting, because we are skipping some of the numbers. Today, we are going to review counting by 2s.

Trace the numbers below, and then fill in the missing numbers. Say the numbers as you write them.

_____ , 1 , _____ , 3 , _____ , 5 ,

_____ , 7 , _____ , 9 , _____

Now write the numbers you filled in without the numbers in between.

_____

- -

_____

Do you remember the Bible story Grandma told Charlie and Charlotte, about the Great Flood and a man named Noah? Re-tell the story to your teacher.

In the space below, draw a picture of animals going into the Ark walking in 2s. Count the animals by 2s. How many did you draw?

Numbers for copywork. Say the numbers out loud as you write them. Find them on your 100's Chart.

0 2 4 6 8 10

12 14 16 18 20

Talk to your teacher about the pattern you see in the numbers above. Look at the last digit of each number. Write the pattern.

_____

Hands-on practice. Line up small counting items or small toys in rows of 2s. Practice skip counting by 2s. Like this.

 1   3   5   7   9

 2   4   6   8   10

Today we are going to practice skip counting by 5s. Trace these numbers and say them out loud.

0 5 10 15 20 25

30 35 40 45 50

Talk to your teacher about the pattern you see.

What do the numbers end in? _____ and _____

On your 100's Chart, place a small counting item on each number as you count by 5s.

Now it's your turn to write the numbers. Cover the numbers at the top of this page and write them from memory. Did you get them all right?

Make a poster showing everything you have learned about skip counting by 2s and 5s. Be creative! When you are finished with your project, show your family or class!

Ideas:

- Use stickers or small pictures from old magazines (or you could draw them!) to show groups of 2s (on one side of the poster) and groups of 5s on the other side.

- Write nice and big! Write the numbers you say when you skip-count by 2s and 5s under the pictures.

Teacher

An alternative to a poster would be to have your student make a book of skip counting. Using the same concepts as the poster, encourage your student to show what they have learned about skip-counting.

1 2 3 4 5 6 7 8

Use this color guide to color the elephant,

Review of Skip Counting 10's & Tally Marks

Tally marks are simple lines that you group together so you can keep count of things. They are usually done in groups of five as you see here. What is the number that the tally marks on the chalkboard add up to?

(Hint! You could count each of the tally marks, but there is a faster way. We know each set of tally marks equal five. So skip count by five for each set. Have you found the answer? That's right! It's 15.)

In our last lesson, we reviewed skip counting by 2s and 5s. In this lesson, we are going to review skip counting by 10s and the use of tally marks.

Trace the numbers.

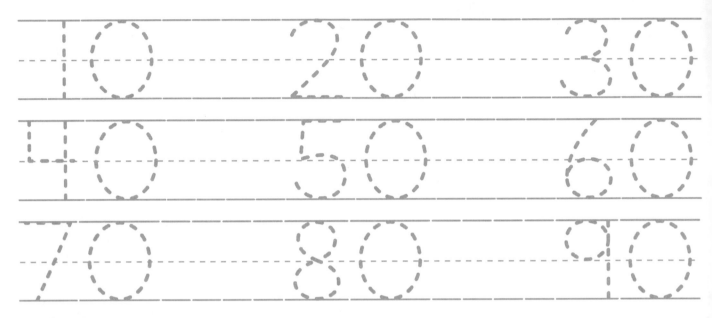

Find the numbers on your 100's Chart. Talk to your teacher about the pattern you see. What does each number end in?

_____

Now cover the numbers at the top of this page and write them from memory.

Did you get them all right? _____

A review of tally marks.

When we use tally marks, we make 1 mark for every object we count. We write 4 marks side by side, and the fifth mark goes across the first 4. Count the objects in each set and make tally marks. The first one is done for you.

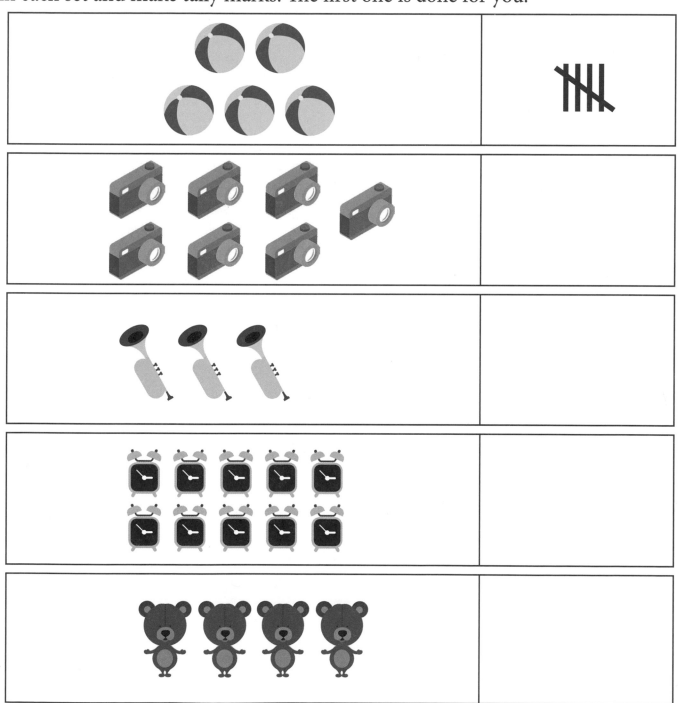

On your 100's Chart, circle the numbers 0–100, skip counting by 10s. Write them here. Say them out loud.

_____

- -

_____

_____

- -

_____

_____

- -

_____

Practice counting groups of 10.

1	2	3	4	5

6	7	8	9	10

Draw the correct number of objects.

4 □ _____

9 ○ _____

7 △ _____

3 ◇ _____

5 ○ _____

8 ▭ _____

2 ⬡ _____

6 ▭ _____

1 ☆ _____

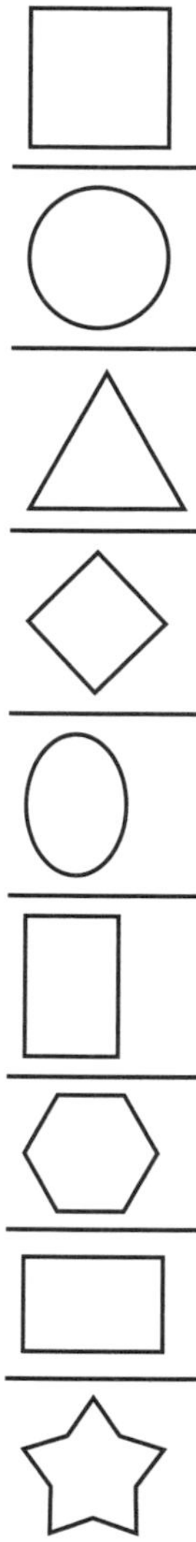

Write the numbers. Skip count by 10s and write the numbers on the lines.

_____

- - - - - - - - - - - - - - - - - -

_____

_____

- - - - - - - - - - - - - - - - - -

_____

Find the numbers on your 100's chart.

Count small counting items into groups of 1–10. On slips of paper, write tally marks to match your groups. Challenge your teacher to a game of matching! Now let them make the groups, and you match them with the right tally marks.

Write the numbers 10–100, skip counting by 10, on small pieces of paper. Shuffle them and put them in order. See how fast you can do it.

Write the numbers here:

Review Time!

Make a poster or a small book to show what you have learned about skip counting by 10s. Use pictures from old magazines, stickers, or drawings to make a book showing what you have learned about tally marks. Have fun with it!

FIND and CIRCLE 2 of THE SAME PICTURES

Review of Numbers to 100

We have reached the last lesson of our book! I hope you have had a wonderful time learning about mathematics this year. In our final lesson we are going to review numbers from 0–100. You are going to be writing sections of numbers every day, and by the end of the week, you will have written all of the numbers 0–100!

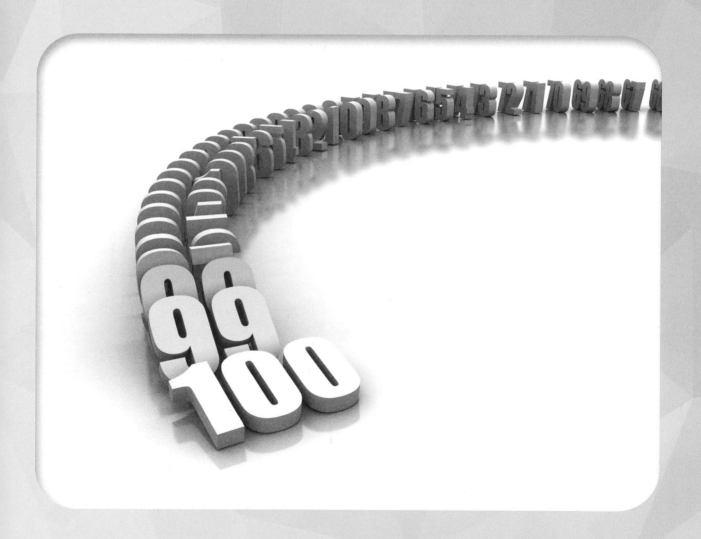

Write the numbers 0–20 from memory. When you are finished, check your numbers with your 100's Chart.

Say the numbers out loud.

Write the numbers 21–40 from memory. When you are finished, check your numbers with your 100's Chart.

Say the numbers out loud.

Write the numbers 41–60 from memory. When you are finished, check your numbers with your 100's Chart.

Say the numbers out loud.

Write the numbers 61–80 from memory. When you are finished, check your numbers with your 100's Chart.

Say the numbers out loud.

Write the numbers 81–100 from memory. When you are finished, check your numbers with your 100's Chart.

_____

- -

_____

_____

- -

_____

_____

- -

_____

_____

- -

_____

Say the numbers out loud.

The End
Congratulations!
You did it!

Manipulatives Section

Manipulatives are simply objects used to teach students through hands-on learning. The manipulatives listed here can be found on the following pages. Below each one are the pages where you can find them mentioned in the book.

- Place Value Village (pages 327 and 329)

  Reference pages: 85, 87, 90, 91, 93, 96–100, 107, 108, 113, 116–118, 121, 124, 125, 131, 139, 142, 158, 183, 189, 192, 193, 199, 205, 219, 228, 256, 265, 293–297

- Place Value Village Counting Mat (page 331)

  Reference pages: 85, 91, 97–100, 116–118, 121, 125, 131, 139, 142, 158, 183, 192, 193, 199, 219, 293–297

- My Addition Mat (horizontal) (page 333)

  Reference pages: 132, 133, 138, 140, 143, 147, 149, 182, 193, 205, 213, 225, 300

- My Addition Mat (vertical) (page 334)

  Reference pages: 155, 182, 193, 213, 302

- Number Cards (page 335)

  Reference pages: 66, 93, 121, 132, 205

- My 100's Chart (page 337)

  Reference pages: 100, 114, 124, 148, 158, 160, 166, 175, 178, 182, 184, 189, 190, 192, 196–198, 200, 202–204, 209, 212, 217–220, 225, 228, 235, 239, 246, 248, 265, 266, 270, 274, 279, 281, 294–298, 307, 308, 312, 314, 315, 320–324

- Days-of-the-Week Cards (page 339)

  Reference pages: 146, 149, 150, 165, 174, 177

- Clock Assembly (page 341)

  Reference pages: 226–228, 233–235, 237–239, 243

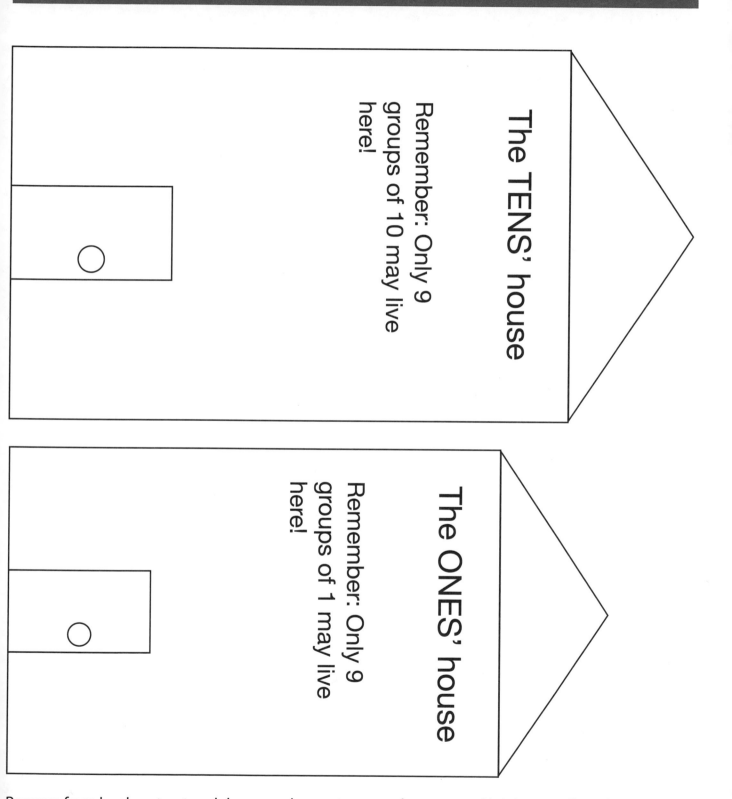

The TENS' house

Remember: Only 9 groups of 10 may live here!

The ONES' house

Remember: Only 9 groups of 1 may live here!

Remove from book, cut out each house, color, paste to sturdy paper, and laminate. Adhere houses to sides of Place Value Village containers.

The HUNDREDS' house

Remember: Only 9 groups of a hundred may live here!

Remove from book, cut out house, color, paste to sturdy paper, and laminate. Adhere house to side of Place Value Village container.

Place Value Village Counting Mat

HUNDREDS	TENS	ONES

Remove from book, trim rough edges, and laminate. Store with your Place Value Village!
Use with washable markers.

My Addition Mat (horizontal side)

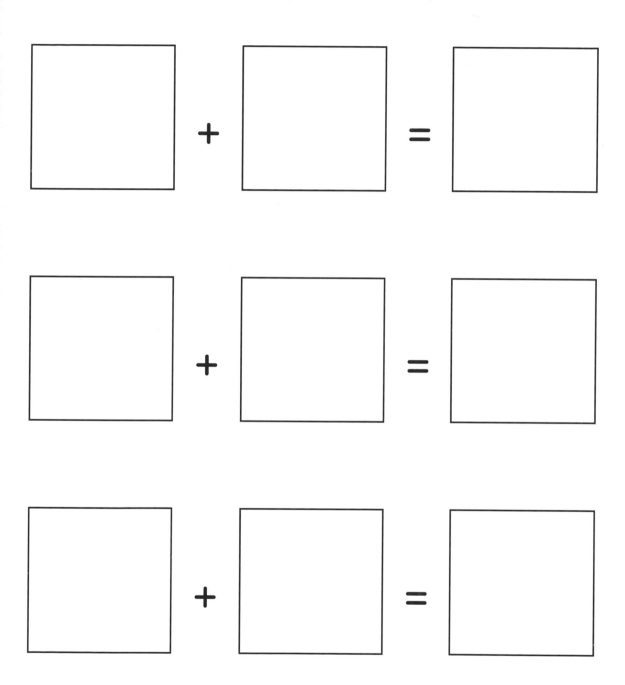

Carefully pull this page out of your book, trim off rough edge and laminate with contact paper.
Use with washable markers.

My Addition Mat (vertical side)

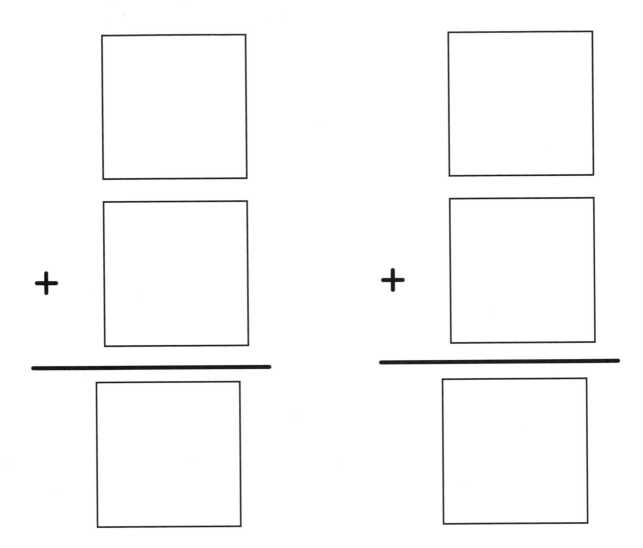

Carefully pull this page out of your book, trim off rough edge and laminate with contact paper.

Math Level 1 – Manipulatives

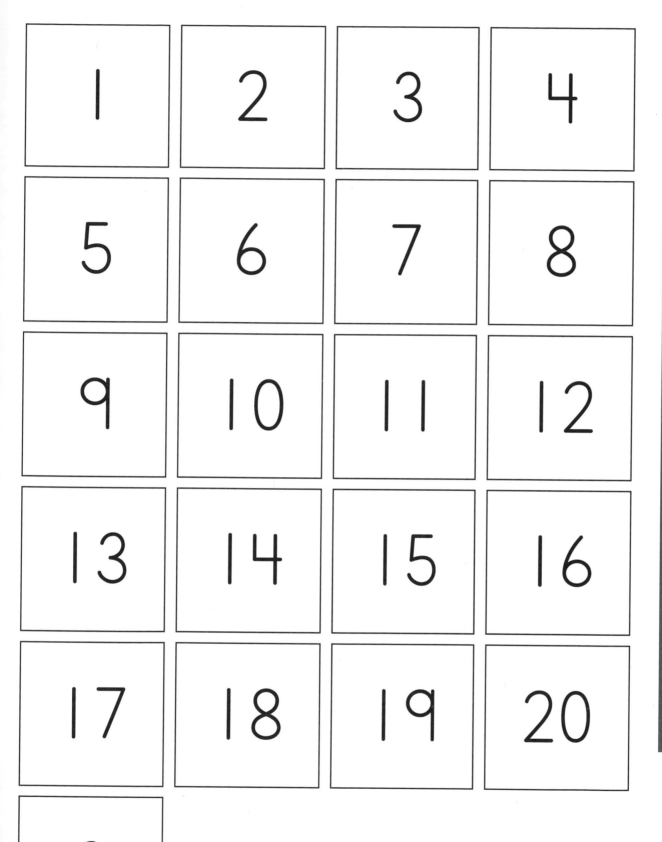

My 100's Chart

0	1	2	3	4	5	6	7	8	9
10	11	12	13	14	15	16	17	18	19
20	21	22	23	24	25	26	27	28	29
30	31	32	33	34	35	36	37	38	39
40	41	42	43	44	45	46	47	48	49
50	51	52	53	54	55	56	57	58	59
60	61	62	63	64	65	66	67	68	69
70	71	72	73	74	75	76	77	78	79
80	81	82	83	84	85	86	87	88	89
90	91	92	93	94	95	96	97	98	99
100									

Directions: Remove from book, trim rough edge and laminate.
Use with washable markers.

My 100's Chart

Directions: Blank chart for you to write on. Remove from book, trim rough edge and laminate. Use with washable markers.

Math Level 1 – Manipulatives

Sunday	Monday
Tuesday	Wednesday
Thursday	Friday

Saturday

Cut out cards and store them in an envelope in your manipulatives container.

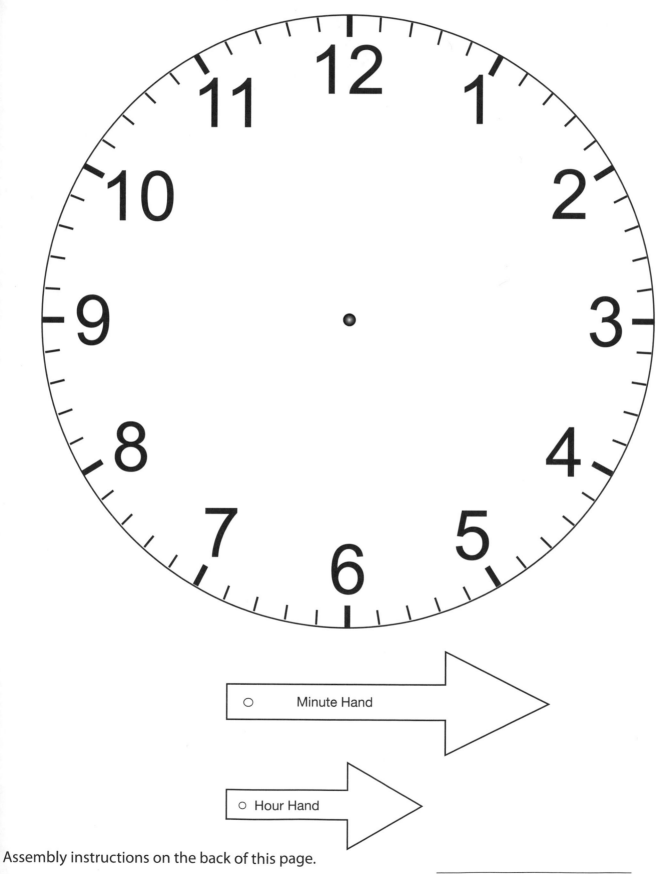

Assembly directions:

Carefully cut out clock and hands. Color the hour hand blue and the minute hand red. Cover each piece with contact paper, and trim close to the edge. With a sharp pencil make a small hole where it is marked in the center of the clock and hands. (ADULTS DO THIS STEP)

Stack the minute hand on the top of the hour hand.

Use a brass fastener to connect the hands to the clock.

Appendix – Bean Sprouting Project Instructions

Gather items listed on page 186.

1. Make sure your jar is clean and dry. (You may use a tall, clear, glass drinking glass, or any other clear glass container if you do not have a quart sized canning jar.)

2. Tear off a piece of white paper towel that is about a yard long, and fold it so that when you place it into the jar, it pushes smoothly against the sides of the jar.

3. Carefully place your bean vertically about half-way down the side of the jar. You want your bean to be as visible as possible through the jar, so make sure you don't place it behind any engraving or writing on the glass.

4. Carefully pour enough water into the jar that the paper towel starts soaking it up (this is usually about $\frac{3}{4}$ cup if you are using a quart jar). Make sure you pour it right down the center of the curled around paper towel. You do not want to get your bean wet! Watch to make sure your paper towel is "drinking" the water.

5. Carefully set your jar in a window sill or a sunny spot.

6. You will have to add water whenever there is no water visible in the bottom of your jar.

7. It usually only takes a few days to start seeing growth in your bean! After it has sprouted and sent down a good root, students may enjoy transplanting the baby bean plant into a pot with potting soil.

Appendix – Right Brain Flashcards

Right brain flashcards teach a concept by giving the "whole" story. Most flashcards are plain-colored and are missing the answer. Right brain flashcards teach a fact by giving the child a story to remember. See the *Math Teaching Companion* for great tips on right brain flashcards.

How to make right brain flashcards

1. Involve your student. Have them help you come up with a funny story that shows a math fact. (Look below for a sample flashcard.)

2. Have students help make their flashcards. We want students to OWN their own education. The sooner they take responsibility for their learning, the better.

3. Use color, texture, and words on your flashcards:

4. Make them double-sided. In this math program, students are going to be making their flashcards with vertical addition on one side and horizontal on the other. Use the same story on both sides.

5. Review often, and have students tell their math stories from their flashcards.

Punch a hole in the card and place it on a ring. It is best to use large index cards.

Flashcard page references:

Flashcard intro: page 155

Review: pages 157, 158, 164-167, 173, 174, 181, 186, 191, 192, 197–199, 205, 212, 225–228, 230, 235, 237–239, 266, 281, 299, 300, 302

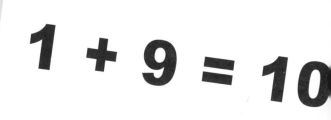

10's family: pages 183, 184

Time cards: pages 243, 246, 247, 249, 253, 254, 265, 281